WITHDRAWN
NDSU

Mounting the Threat

Mounting the Threat

THE BATTLE OF BOURGUEBUS RIDGE,
18–23 JULY 1944

JOHN J. T. SWEET

SAN RAFAEL • CALIFORNIA

D
756.5
B65
S85

Copyright © 1977 by
Presidio Press
1114 Irwin Street
San Rafael, California 94901

Library of Congress Catalog Card Number: 77-073555
ISBN: 0-89141-026-0

Cover and book design by James Mennick
Printed in the United States of America

For my parents

Foreword

"Operation Goodwood" was a controversial battle from every aspect. Its object, its tactics, and its results have all been hotly argued in military circles over the past thirty years.

The author of this book has made a most painstaking and thorough research into all the different statements that have been made and views which have been expressed, and has, I believe, come to a sound conclusion on the broad issues. As one of the leading participants of the battle, I am naturally very glad that this has been done and am grateful to Mr. Sweet for his thorough investigation.

For myself, I can state definitely that I was quite clear that the Bourguebus Ridge was our main objective and anything beyond that was a hope, and surely one must always be hopeful in war.

I think it is interesting to note that although 11th Armoured Division had such very heavy tank casualties, the results achieved by the operation had maintained the morale to such an extent that within nine days of the conclusion of Goodwood, we took part in one of our most successful battles of the campaign at Caumont, in the "bocage" country, and were in Antwerp five weeks later.

> G.P.B. Roberts
> Major General
> Commander 11th Armoured Division
> 1943–45

Preface

IN THIS ATTEMPT to write a clear and accurate account of Operation Goodwood, methodology and sources have been great problems. This book was to be, and hopefully is, an account with most of the available material completely and correctly evaluated. Most of the sources were published material, i.e., regimental histories and other narratives. I was also very lucky to be able to attend the 1971 Staff College Battlefield Tour of the Operation Goodwood area, meet many of the major participants and view the actual battlefield. I was fortunate to be allowed to see two copies of the original *British Army of the Rhine Battlefield Tour* book, which has been used by virtually every other author. One copy was in the Chester Wilmot Papers in the Liddell Hart Library and, by examining these, I was able to form a more accurate opinion of the value of *The*

Struggle for Europe than is prevalent among many historians. The only major sources I was unable to see were the British war diaries which remained under the thirty years' restriction rule and the Canadian war diaries which were available only in Ottawa.

The number of very helpful people I met was perhaps the most beneficial part of the project. Chief among these must be Lieutenant Colonel W.B.R. Neave-Hill of the Historical Section, British Ministry of Defence Library. Colonel Neave-Hill went to great lengths to assist in my research and provide not only material that would have been otherwise unavailable but also his own great expertise on the subject.

Major C.W.G. Bullocke of the British Staff College, Camberley, was also most helpful. In addition to providing Staff College material, he enabled me to attend the battlefield tour. During the actual tour, Lietutenant Colonel Alister Dennis was most helpful, and I owe a particularly heavy debt to Major General G.P.B. Roberts who went out of his way to answer my questions and lend me material I would not have otherwise been able to study in detail. I can only hope that this analysis does justice to his role in these events.

In the United States, Professors Charles Burdick and George Moore were very generous with their time and knowledge. To them I owe a particular debt for their support and interest.

Acknowledgments

I WOULD LIKE to acknowledge the kindness of the following authors and publishers in granting permission to quote from their respective books: Simon and Schuster, Inc. for *My Three Years with Eisenhower*, copyright 1946 by Harry C. Butcher; Charles Scribner's Sons for Major General Sir Francis de Guingand, *Operation Victory*; Her Majesty's Stationery Office for L.F. Ellis, *Victory in the West*; Gale and Polden Limited for L.F. Ellis, *The Welsh Guards at War*, and D.J.L. FitzGerald, *History of the Irish Guards in the Second World War*; and Holt, Rinehart and Winston for Omar N. Bradley, *A Soldier's Story*.

Also, the Scots Guards for D.H. Erskine, *The Scots Guards*; Ralph Ingersoll for his book, *Top Secret*; G.S. Jackson for his book, *Operations Eight Corps*; the estate of the late Viscount Montgomery of Alamein for Vis-

G. P. Putnam's Sons for *The Memoirs of Field Marshal Montgomery*, copyright 1958 by Viscount Montgomery of Alamein; William Collins, Sons & Co., Ltd., for Norman Scarfe, *Assault Division*; Little, Brown and Company for Lord Tedder, *With Prejudice*; and the Harold Matson Co., Inc. for *The Struggle for Europe*, copyright 1952 by Chester Wilmot.

The quotations from Frederick Morgan's *Overture to Overlord* are reprinted by permission of A.D. Peters and Co. Ltd. The quotations from J.B. Salmond's *The History of the 51st Highland Division 1939-1945* are reprinted with the permission of William Blackwood & Sons Ltd. Those from C.P. Stacey's *The Victory Campaign* are reproduced by permission of the Minister of Supply and Services, Canada.

The maps of the battle are reproduced by the kind permission of the commandant of the Staff College, Camberley.

Contents

Foreword		vii
Preface		ix
Acknowledgments		xi
Introduction		xv
I.	Planning the Normandy Invasion	1
II.	The Battle for the Beachhead	17
III.	Operation Goodwood: The Plan	33
IV.	The Opposing Forces	49
V.	The Battle: First Day	67
VI.	Conclusion of the Battle	89
VII.	The Threat is Mounted	107
	Appendix A: Allied Chain of Command	124
	Appendix B: Allied Formations	125
	Appendix C: German Order of Battle	130
	Appendix D: Weapon Comparison	131
	Bibliography	133
	Index	139

Maps

1.	General Orientation Map	5
2.	Caen and Vicinity	11
3.	Enemy Defenses	63
4.	Situation, 0500 Hours, 18 July	80
5.	Situation, 1100 Hours	85
6.	Situation, 1100-1900 Hours	92
7.	Situation, 19 July	103

Illustrations

	following page
The Leaders	36
The Weapons	54
The Battle	100

(Photographs courtesy of the Imperial War Museum, London, England)

Introduction

THE MASSIVE BRITISH armoured attack, Operation Goodwood, was important both as an essential part of the Allied campaign for the liberation of northwest Europe in 1944 and as a major influence on armoured doctrine. It is mentioned in virtually every history of the period, albeit with frequent mistakes and little understanding, and is a major study of students at the British army's Staff College at Camberley, Surrey. Goodwood is considered so important that each year the Staff College students attend a battlefield tour conducted by various surviving commanders, involving a bus tour and seven briefings on different stages of the battle held at vantage points on the field.

This study, like the battlefield tour, has as its purpose the discussion of Operation Goodwood from conception to conclusion. It is not intended to be a history of the Invasion and the Normandy campaign but only of the British operations on the extreme left flank of the Allied Expeditionary Force which led to the British army being on Bourguebus Ridge by 23 July 1944. The entire campaign with the complexities of national pride and conflict are well covered by others, and it is the intention of this author to mention wider considerations only when they have direct bearing on Operation Goodwood and basically to neglect the American front.

Similarly, I rely more heavily on British sources since they were closer to the events. The British authors are without exception more opinionated and much less tactful than their American contemporaries. It is the interpretation of this author, based on study of the entire body of literature, that the British are more honest than the Americans in their presentation of interpersonal relations and animosities. The American authors are polite and gentlemanly about most situations, but having served as a staff officer in an American unit in combat, I am convinced that no group of senior United States officers could conduct any operation without the interpersonal conflict and hostility the British imply and the Americans deny.

Before moving on to Goodwood, a brief outline of the entire campaign will serve as a useful background to the coming events. For a variety of political and strategic reasons, a final front for the defeat of Germany, involving Anglo-American forces, had to be created in western Europe. With the English Channel coast of France the only reasonable target, the Normandy coastline was chosen by the Allied high command, for reasons covered in Chapter I. Following the landings, the strategic plan called for a sweep northeastward from the lodgement area on a wide front into Belgium and the Netherlands and to the Franco-German border. An additional landing in the south of France would protect that flank, while the sea would protect the other.

The Channel ports and Antwerp would be captured to serve as supply bases, and the major portion of Belgium and France along with southeastern Holland would be liberated. When this firm base was available, the final blow would be launched against the strategic north German plain with its vital cities and broad avenues of movement. This last attack would be launched on a broad front from the Ardennes to the Arnhem-Nijmegen area by the massed armies of the western Allies. The "Victory Campaign," as the Canadian official history calls it, actually followed this course of events, but only after many changes, such as those caused by the Battle of the Falaise Gap and the Battle of the Bulge.[1]

---

1. Dwight D. Eisenhower, *Crusade in Europe*, has on pages 229-31 a brief discussion of the plan along with two maps which are very clear. *The Administrative History of the Operations of 21 Army Group on the Continent of Europe, 6 June 1944–48 May 1945* has voluminous appendices showing requirements for these operations and the elaborate mechanism required to keep everything functioning, and is the best source on what was needed for the breakout.

Many of the most important changes occurred during the initial phase, while the Allied Expeditionary Force was still confined to the beachhead. The initial plan had been to build strength on the beachhead, defeat the enemy there, and then begin the advance. The plan for the Battle of Normandy was a series of alternating attacks by the two (British and American) flanks until the enemy could be defeated and then a sweep by the American flank, swinging on the British hinge at Caen, eastward toward the German frontier, and thus outflanking the German defenders. Stiff German resistance and the consequent failure to gain expected territory caused delays and readjustments in this part of the plan and provoked controversy.

The first controversies concerned whether the British army was doing its part in the campaign. Criticism from a variety of sources was focused on the British ground commander, General Montgomery, since he was, of course, responsible for all that his command did or failed to do. In addition he was an aggressive and difficult personality, who was perhaps overeager to claim credit for any victory. However, the author believes that in this early controversy, unlike later ones involving Montgomery's strategy and tactics, the situation which developed before the British front was the result of events largely beyond his control. Such factors as reinforcements, supplies and German resistance, combined with misunderstandings by Allied commanders over stated objectives and plans, were responsible for the slowness of movement by the British forces rather than errors of judgment by Montgomery or anyone else. Although American sources play down this early conflict, the author feels the evidence produced in Chapters VI and VII shows that there was substantial ill feeling over Montgomery's actions in June and July 1944.

The purpose then will be twofold: to recount the events on the British front from the planning stages through the conclusion of Goodwood, and to describe and discuss the inter-Allied controversy that occurred over General Montgomery's conduct of the Normandy campaign through Operation Goodwood.

CHAPTER I

Planning the Normandy Invasion

ON 18 JULY 1944, preceded by a massive aerial and artillery bombardment, three-fourths of the armoured divisions of the British army attacked south from the Normandy beachhead against strong German defensive positions. This was Operation Goodwood. Bourguebus Ridge, a major terrain feature southwest of Caen, was their objective, with further exploitation south and east toward Falaise and Paris, their next objective, as a possible bonus.[1] Three days later, this attack, the most massive British armoured operation since El Alamein, had ended, drowned in summer rain and rising criticism. General Sir Bernard Montgomery's[2] massive attack had gained five miles of Normandy cornfield,

---

1. All geographic references are to Maps 1 to 4, which are progressively larger-scale maps of the area of operations.
2. General Montgomery was promoted to Field Marshal on 1 September 1944. Although I have tried to use the correct title, i.e., general, occasionally a quotation may use the later rank.

inflicted heavy casualties on the German defenders, and caused major readjustments in the distribution of German forces opposing the Allies. These important achievements, which had a major influence on future operations, were overshadowed by a major inter-Allied controversy over General Montgomery and his conduct of Goodwood.

Coalition warfare is always a tenuous operation, but, in the case of the Anglo-American Allied Expeditionary Force, public opinion and personality conflicts were to magnify the inherent possibilities for misunderstanding. While nationality tended to be the major distinction in the Goodwood controversy, command relations and interservice rivalry were also causes of the trouble.

The main questions were the relative degree of participation in combat by the two Allies, and Montgomery's intentions and responsibilities. General Dwight D. Eisenhower, the Supreme Commander; some American observers, such as General Omar Bradley, Captain Harry Butcher, and Ralph Ingersoll; and several high ranking officers of the Royal Air Force, especially Air Chief Marshal Tedder, believed after the first day of the battle, and have continued to feel, that Montgomery promised a great deal more success from Goodwood than he delivered from the attack. They also considered Montgomery's entire conduct of the campaign after the invasion to have lacked aggressiveness and achievement. This criticism was widespread among American commanders and has been perpetuated in many American books.[3] Virtually all British army personnel, from Montgomery's

---

3. For example, see Omar N. Bradley, *A Soldier's Story*, pp. 325-26, and Harry C. Butcher, *My Three Years with Eisenhower*. For British criticism, Lord Tedder, *With Prejudice*, is aptly titled.

immediate subordinates to the infantry riflemen, supported him. The British believed that, given the situation, Montgomery did very well. They considered that the Americans disregarded his stated intentions, the extremely effective German resistance, the tenuous manpower situation of the British who were virtually without reinforcements, and the fact that Montgomery did indeed plan and carry out a major victory.

The command conflicts, and the fact that Goodwood was the first large tank battle in western Europe after the invasion, make the operation an interesting and informative phase in the history of the liberation of Europe. Goodwood is, moreover, an excellent example of the problems of both inter-Allied cooperation and armoured warfare.

In order to understand Operation Goodwood and the criticism of General Montgomery's conduct of the battle, one must look briefly at the planning and conduct of the Normandy campaign prior to 18 July 1944.

The initial planning for the invasion of Normandy was carried out, in fact, long before General Montgomery arrived on the scene. On 15 July 1943, Lieutenant General Sir Fredrick Morgan, Chief of Staff to the Supreme Allied Commander (designate), COSSAC,[4] submitted a plan for the invasion of northwestern Europe to the British chiefs of staff. COSSAC, as both Morgan and his planning staff were known, had been charged by the Combined Chiefs of Staff on 26 April 1943 with planning operations to

---

4. Lt. Gen. Sir Fredrick Morgan, *Overture to Overlord*, p. 155. The title "Chief of Staff to the Supreme Allied Commander (designate)" was used to indicate the absence of a commander.

defeat the Germans in northwest Europe. In addition, the staff was charged with conditions as to date, preparation, and general structure of the proposed operations. The COSSAC plan, called Overlord, designated the Normandy coast between the mouth of the River Orne and the base of the Cotentin Peninsula as the initial landing area. This area was chosen by COSSAC over other possible locations, especially the Pas de Calais which seemed the logical choice, for three reasons: first, the Caen-Cotentin area on the Baie de la Seine was relatively lightly defended; second, it possessed good terrain for the landing and for the construction of airfields needed to support continental operations; and third, the area was close to the ports of Cherbourg and the Brittany Peninsula, the use of which would be required for any sustained operations.[5]

The planned invasion beaches lie along a coast which runs east-west between the Seine estuary on the east and the Cotentin Peninsula on the west. The main beaches lie between two rivers: the Vire on the west, running north-south at the base of the Cotentin; and the Orne-Odon system, running from the coast southwest, isolating the beaches from the Falaise area. The beaches themselves are backed by open areas that end in a series of ridges, the beginning of the interior highlands, which restrict movement of major forces. These ridges, beginning seven to fifteen miles from the beaches, have limited road networks and contain few urban areas. The major population centers are situated in the river valleys just in front of the ridge system. These cities, St. Lo and Caen, were to be crucial objectives in the early stages of the Invasion.

---

5. Field Marshal the Viscount Montgomery of Alamein, *Normandy to the Baltic*, pp. 8-9.

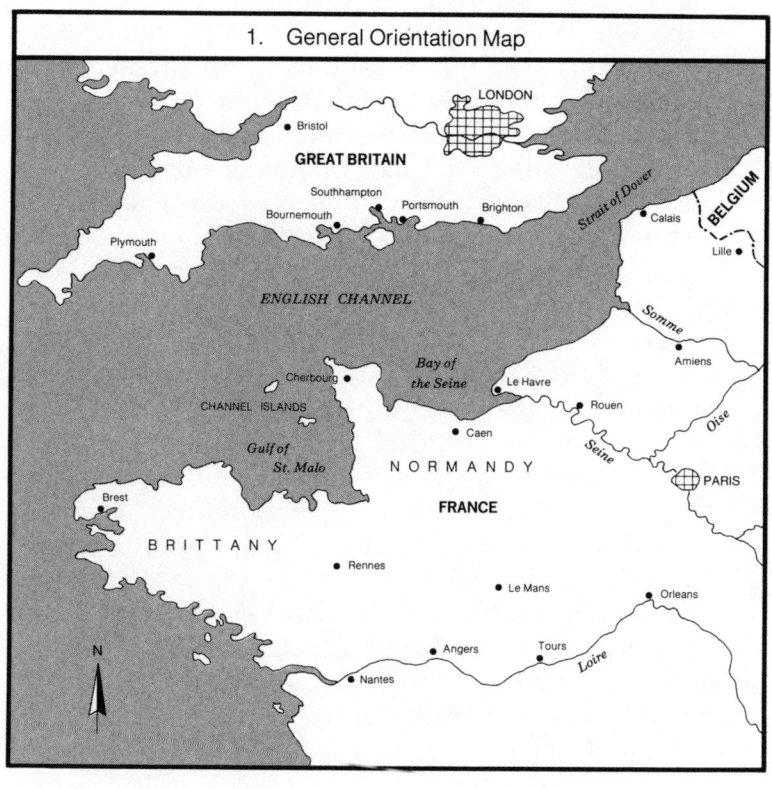

1. General Orientation Map

St. Lo, on the Vire roughly fifteen miles inland, was the communications center on the American front; and Caen, on the Orne just where the Odon branches off and seven miles from the coast, was the British sector's communications hub.[6]

From Caen three basic avenues of movement were available: east toward Lisieux, south along the valley of the Orne, or southeast along Bourguebus Ridge which was between the two and by far the best choice. By following the ridge from Caen to Falaise, the military commander would find gentle terrain with a good road as the center axis, no major obstacles and, especially, no large rivers to cross. From Falaise the same basic situation exists east to Paris and the Seine. The routes to Lisieux and along the Orne Valley are both less desirable because of obstacles like the Dives and Tocques rivers and the steep sides of Mt. Picon and the Orne Valley. All three avenues were tried by the British in the days after the invasion, but both sides realized the importance of Bourguebus Ridge. The final success of the Allies was a result of the capture of the Bourguebus Ridge-Falaise area. Success was achieved two months from the day Caen was initially scheduled to be taken.

Having arrived at a basic plan of operations and target area, the Combined Chiefs of Staff now required a commander and staff to carry out these operations.[7] At the Quebec Conference in August 1943, the United States agreed to have British officers as

---

6. The terrain analysis is based on map reconnaissance of the area using the maps in L. F. Ellis, *Victory in the West: Vol. 1. The Battle of Normandy*, and C. P. Stacey, *The Victory Campaign*, and 1/50,000 scale maps published by L'Institut Geographique National, Paris.
7. See Appendix A, "Allied Chain of Command."

naval and air commanders, but the planners dropped the previous idea of a British Supreme Commander, since it had become clear that the majority of participating troops would be American.[8] Churchill then graciously proposed that an American should be appointed to this post. After some further juggling of details, President Roosevelt appointed General Dwight D. Eisenhower as Supreme Commander, with a British air chief marshal as his assistant. A second position, that of ground commander for the Invasion, was to be a temporary position filled by the British army group commander, General Sir Bernard Montgomery.[9]

Both Eisenhower and Montgomery, who had been in high positions in the Mediterranean theater, arrived in England in January 1944. Eisenhower had been Supreme Allied Commander in the Mediterranean, and Montgomery had been the commander of the British Eighth Army, originally a separate command under Alexander, but from the invasion of Sicily onward, subordinate to Eisenhower's command. In fact the two men had occupied positions similar to those they would be taking over, except that Montgomery had not commanded any American troops in Italy.

---

8. Stacey, *Victory Campaign*, p. 19.
9. Winston S. Churchill, *The Second World War: Closing the Ring*, p. 423. Montgomery was not, in fact, Eisenhower's first choice. He preferred Sir Harold Alexander, who was his deputy in the Mediterranean, but the British refused to release Alexander. See Dwight D. Eisenhower, *Crusade in Europe*, p. 31 and Omar N. Bradley, *A Soldier's Story*, pp. 207-9: there seems to be a little hostility shown in both books over not having Alexander, especially with reference to the personalities of the two candidates.

On arrival, the Combined Chiefs of Staff gave Eisenhower his task:

> You will enter the Continent of Europe and, in conjunction with the other United Nations, undertake operations aimed at the heart of Germany and the destruction of her armed forces. The date for entering the Continent is the month of May, 1944. After adequate Channel ports have been secured, exploitation will be directed towards securing an area that will facilitate both ground and air operations against the enemy.[10]

To implement this directive, Caen became a major objective of the Normandy operations.

General Morgan felt "from the first moment that the command objective of supreme importance was the town of Caen with its command of communications." To achieve this goal he stated, "We judged the importance of Caen to be such that the bulk of the available airborne troops, whatever that might turn out to be, should be allotted to assist in its capture." The next objective should be "good ground for airfields southeastward from Caen."[11] The task of turning the plans of COSSAC into tactical reality fell to General Montgomery,[12] who would command all

---

10. Ellis, *Victory in the West*, p. 499, Appendix 1, Directive to Supreme Allied Expeditionary Forces (issued February 12, 1944), paragraph 2.
11. Morgan, *Overture to Overlord*, p. 159.
12. Montgomery technically was to remain "ground forces commander" until 1 September 1944, although after the establishment of 12th U. S. Army Group on 1 August, Bradley was to all intents and purposes coequal with Montgomery. See R. W. Thompson, *Montgomery, The Field Marshal*, pp. 99-100, 105.

ground forces in the landing. Montgomery, along with many other commanders who saw the COSSAC plan, thought that it needed substantial changes. Some adjustments had been made by COSSAC before Montgomery arrived, but he formulated the modifications to the original plan that were actually used on D day.[13]

Beginning with his arrival in January and culminating in a 7 April 1944 briefing, Montgomery altered the plan in three respects: a wider frontage attack, increased unit strength in the assault and subsequent buildup, and changes in the chain of command.[14] On 17 April the new and, in general, final plan was unveiled:

> The British Second Army, after assaulting to the west of the Orne River, was to develop operations to the south and southeast in order to secure airfield sites, and to protect the eastern flank of the First U.S. Army while it was capturing Cherbourg. In its subsequent operations the Army was to pivot on its left flank and offer a strong front against enemy movement toward the lodgement area from the east.[15]

---

13. Of course, many people contributed to the plan, as it was drawn up by Montgomery's staff; but Montgomery was the responsible commander, the man who made the decisions. Eisenhower, *Crusade in Europe*, pp. 228, 243-44, covers this fairly well. Bradley, *A Soldier's Story*, p. 221, gives insight into how the planning was actually done, and pp. 236-41 acknowledge Montgomery's responsibility for the plan.
14. Major General Sir Francis de Guingand, *Operation Victory*, p. 344.
15. *Ibid.*, pp. 377-78.

Montgomery elaborated:

> Once ashore and firmly established, my plan was to threaten to break out of the initial bridgehead on the eastern flank—that is in the Caen sector. I intended by means of this threat to draw the main enemy reserves into that sector to fight them there and keep them there, using the British and Canadian armies for the purpose. Having got the main enemy reserves committed on the eastern flank, my plan was to make the break-out on the western flank, using for this task the American armies under General Bradley, and to pivot the whole front on Caen. The American break-out thrust was to be delivered southwards down to the Loire and then to be developed eastwards in a wide sweep up to the Seine about Paris. This movement was designed to cut off all the enemy forces south of the Seine, over which river the bridges were to be destroyed by air action.[16]

Montgomery gave as reasons for this plan, the "layout of enemy reserve formations in western Europe, the run of rail and road communications leading to Normandy and the immediate task of the operations: which was to secure ports."[17] The ports, of course, lay to the west of Caen, along the Cotentin Peninsula and in Brittany. Montgomery felt that "on the eastern flank, acquisition of ground was not so pressing providing the Air Force requirements for airfield construction could be met."[18] Much of the later controversy over Montgomery's generalship in

---

16. Montgomery, *Normandy to the Baltic*, p. 21.
17. *Ibid.*
18. *Ibid.*

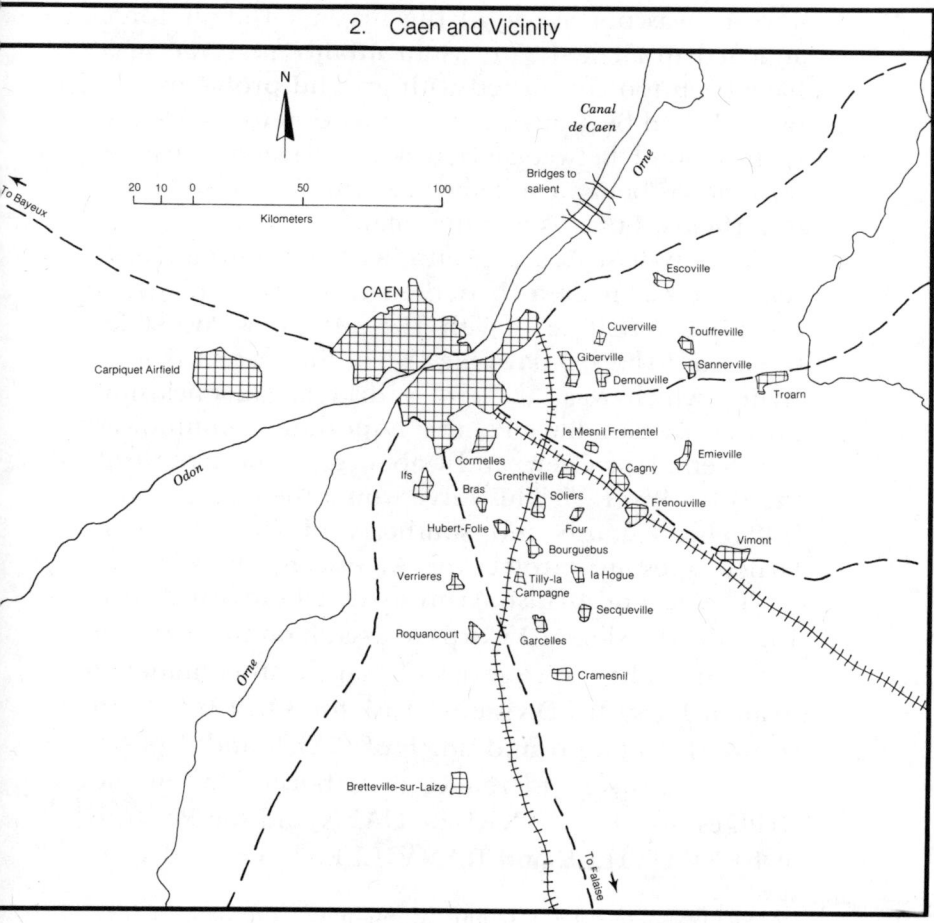

2. Caen and Vicinity

the Normandy campaign centers on this problem. Did Montgomery meet or even try to meet the air force requirements, which would have involved seizure of large areas east of Caen? Apparently Montgomery was not aware of the urgency the air force attached to airfields, or, as an infantryman, he may have been too concerned with ground problems. He said, "It had been my original intention to secure the high ground between Caen and Falaise as early as possible, as being a suitable area for the construction of airfields; but this was not vital."[19]

Twenty-first Army Group, with a requirement to seize the Caen area, had then to prepare plans to accomplish that task with the resources available. Caen was to be a D-day objective of the Second British Army, which was "to seize a bridgehead enclosing Port-en-Bessin, Bayeux, the important communications center of Caen, and Cabourg, at the mouth of the Dives River."[20] This force would then expand the bridgehead south and southeast of Caen to gain airfield sites and protect the Americans' flank.

The Second British Army assigned the 3rd British Infantry Division of I Corps to assault on the extreme left flank. The entire series of plans thus culminated in an order to 3rd Division: "Task for 3 Brit Inf Div to secure the high ground north of CAEN and if possible, CAEN itself; to relieve 6 Airborne Div on the Bridges over the CANAL de CAEN and the R. Orne at BENOUVILLE and RANVILLE."[21] The 3rd Brit-

---

19. Field Marshal the Viscount Montgomery of Alamein, *The Memoirs of Field Marshal Montgomery*, p. 231.
20. Stacey, *Victory Campaign*, p. 72.
21. G1 (ops) Records, 21st Army Group, *Notes on the Operations of 21st Army Group*, p. 6, quoted in Norman Scarfe, *Assault Division*, p. 53.

ish Infantry Division planners selected the 185th Infantry Brigade to take the objectives in this area, making this brigade the first troops committed to the battles around Caen.

The initial attempt to capture Caen on D day failed, largely as the result of the unexpected presence of the German 21st Panzer Division in front of Caen. The 185th Infantry Brigade suffered heavy casualties by mid-afternoon on D day and finally halted some four miles short of the objective.

In accordance with the overall plan, Montgomery during the next two months planned a series of attacks on the two flanks of the lodgement—those on the British flank, to draw the bulk of the German forces, and those on the American, to gain operational room—and then to break out through the weakened German opposition. These attacks would expand the beachhead to allow time and room to build up an adequate supply stockpile and a major striking force for the eventual breakthrough. The attacks took the form of a series of limited operations on either side of Caen: two of the attacks, Operation Charnwood and Operation Windsor, were directed against Caen and its airfield, Carpiquet, while Operations Perch and Epsom were to outflank Caen. At the conclusion of Charnwood on 10 July 1944, the main part of Caen, i.e., all that lay north of the Orne and Odon rivers, was in British hands. However, this meant only that Caen was divided between the two hostile forces and that neither side could use it. Therefore, another attack, to be code-named Goodwood, to reach the high ground southeast of Caen was given the highest priority by Montgomery.

The 21st Army Group planned Operation Goodwood between 10–17 July 1944, and Second British Army[22] carried out the operation between 18–23 July 1944, under the command of Lieutenant General Sir Miles Dempsey. The units involved were three British armoured divisions, a British airborne division in a ground role, two British infantry divisions, and two Canadian infantry divisions.[23] General Dempsey organized these formations into three corps: VIII Corps, commanded by Lieutenant General Sir Richard O'Connor, with the three armoured divisions; I Corps, led by Lieutenant General J. T. Crocker, with the remaining British divisions; and II Canadian Corps, composed of the Canadian divisions under a Canadian commander, Lieutenant General G. G. Simonds. The Second Army assigned each corps its task. The VIII Corps would make the major assault, I Corps on the eastern flank would make a minor atlack in support of the major effort, and II Canadian Corps on the western flank would make a supplementary attack from Caen toward the western end of Bourguebus Ridge. The Canadians were to capture the southern suburbs of Caen—Vaucelles and Cormelles—in the process. The VIII Corps, advancing on Colombelles through Cuverville and Demouville toward the area Bourguebus-Tilly la Campagne, on Bourguebus Ridge, would capture the ridge and then exploit any advantage toward Falaise. The major attack was launched by the British on 18

---

22. The Second British Army was alternatively named the British Liberation Army or BLA, which may appear in some quotations or sources.
23. See Appendix B, "Allied Formations."

July, and by that night casualties and stiffening enemy opposition brought an end to the idea of a major breakthrough by the heavily depleted armoured divisions. On the nineteenth, the attackers launched minor attacks and consolidated the captured area. The armoured divisions were withdrawn by Dempsey on the twentieth, while the Canadians "tidied up" the front line by removing a salient on the right flank. Heavy rains began that day and precluded further large-scale operations. Consolidation operations continued for three days, ending on the twenty-third.

Immediately after Operation Goodwood, with the bulk of German armour facing the British in the Bourguebus Ridge area, Bradley's Americans, with sufficient support available to them, thrust south and then east toward Paris.[24] In the original plan this should have signaled a general advance as the outflanked Germans were forced to readjust their lines to the new situation. At Hitler's order, however, the German forces attempted an attack tg cut off the Americans and were virtually destroyed by the Allies in the Battle of the Falaise Gap. This battle broke German resistance in Normandy and lead to the totally unexpected capture of Antwerp and Brussels within three months of the Invasion. The strategy of "mounting the threat to Falaise"[25] as a key to the German positions in Normandy proved successful by any definition.

---

24. Details on the buildup can be found in *The Administrative History of the Operations of 21 Army Group on the Continent of Europe 6 June 1944–8 May 1945* or, in less complete form, in any of the official histories.
25. Montgomery, *Normandy to the Baltic*, p. 132.

CHAPTER II

The Battle for the Beachhead

THE BATTLES FOR Caen began at 0725 hours on the morning of the 6 June 1944 when lead companies of the 3rd British Division landed at Sword Beach, the easternmost of the D-day beaches. Sword ran from St. Aubin sur Mer to Ouistreham at the mouth of the Orne River. Ten miles to the north lay "Poland," the potential D-day objective of the 3rd Division, which had been revealed as Caen after the troops were on board the invasion ship.

The 3rd Division was returning to France after a four-year absence, its troops in somewhat better order than when they left Dunkirk in 1940; the division commander at Dunkirk, an obscure major general named Bernard Montgomery, was no longer obscure although he still controlled the destiny of the division. The division had been assigned a particularly difficult task which was to involve deeply their former commander. Caen, the communication center of the British front, was to be a major point of contention in the Normandy campaign. The Divisional Intelligence Summary for the 3rd Division had stated, "Caen is likely to be stubbornly defended by the Germans within the limits of the forces at their disposal."[1] Finding out exactly what the "limits of the forces at their disposal" would be, was to take 21st Army Group a very long time.

The battle for Caen became the focal point of British action and American criticism. None of the critics were infantry platoon leaders of the 3rd British or 3rd Canadian Infantry Divisions or the 6th British Airborne Division on D day. Men who had to fight through those ten miles of Norman cornfield to Caen knew why the city did not fall until 18 July.

After the initial D-day gains, a series of vicious and bloody battles for the Caen area ensued, each contributing to the final victory.[2] These battles known as Operations Perch, Epsom and Windsor, were de-

---

1. Norman Scarfe, *Assault Division*, p. 66.
2. This period of the Battle for Normandy is covered in virtually every source, and there is little conflict on the course of events. My discussion is based on L. F. Ellis, *Victory in the West, Vol. 1. The Battle of Normandy*, and C. P. Stacey, *The Victory Campaign*. Contemporary popular accounts can be found in Ross Munro, *Gauntlet to Overlord*, and C. P. Stacey, *Canada's Battle in Normandy*. Modern popular accounts vary greatly in quality, but Eversley Belfield and H. Essame, *The Battle for Normandy*, and Alexander McKee, *Caen, The Anvil of Victory*, are very good. The classic *The Struggle for Europe* by Chester Wilmot is virtually as detailed as the official histories and has influenced all later historians by its copious details and firm opinions.

signed to capture the Caen area by outflanking the defenders. The attacks struck either from the right-hand section of the British front south and southeast behind Caen, or southward behind Caen from that portion of the left flank known as the "airborne salient" after its D-day attackers. The final attack, Operation Charnwood, which captured Caen, wasia frontal assault.

The first of the three attacks, Operation Perch, on 12-13 June, was primarily on the right flank where two divisions were employed, although a third division made a minor attack on the left flank. This pincer attack made only minor gains. Operation Epsom was supposed to follow immediately but was delayed by bad weather. It was finally launched by four divisions on 29 June with no great success. The primary offensive was accompanied by minor attacks in the airborne salient and at Caen airport near the village of Carpiquet. Since the minor assaults were planned to take advantage of the disruption caused by Epsom itself, no more came of them than of the main effort. Operation Windsor, the first all-Canadian assault, followed on 4 July. This third attack was directed against Carpiquet airfield. It placed the Canadian troops on large parts of the airfield, where they held off several counterattacks. On 8–9 July, immediately after Windsor, another British attack was made directly against Caen. This next assault, Operation Charnwood, finally captured all of Caen north of the Orne-Odon river system and made substantial ground gains. It had been a month since the first attack on Normandy.

The fighting for Caen began as the 6th Airborne, the first British formation to reach Normandy, landed early on the morning of 6 June. The troops landed on what was to be the extreme left (eastern flank) of the British invasion with instructions to secure vital bridges and to act as a blocking force against the expected German reinforcements who might counterattack from the Lisieux area to the east. The area that the 6th Airborne was to secure was extensive, from the Orne southeast to Troarn, a town which was not to fall until the general collapse of the German front some two months later. This position would not have been a projecting salient if the 3rd British and the 3rd Canadian Divisions had captured their objectives, roughly along the road from Caen to Bayeux. The British initial assault consisted of the following divisions landing in line from left to right—6th Airborne, 3rd Canadian, and 50th British Infantry Divisions. Later in the day, 51st Highland Division and 7th Armoured Division began landing in the areas that the lead divisions had cleared of Germans.

The troops pushed inland as planned on D day but met with fierce resistance all along the front. The major German counterattack occurred on the boundary between the 3rd British and 3rd Canadian Divisions where an armoured column of the 21st Panzer Division drove a deep wedge. Although disorganization and lack of strength precluded a major German success in the Caen area, a series of events also prevented the British from mounting a serious threat to Caen on D day. On the 6th Airborne Division front, problems developed from the beginning. The British air drop was scattered and most of the troops who were dropped in the area beyond the Orne bridges were too disorganized to have any success against the strong resistance. By midnight on the sixth, the paratroops held the lower Orne and a salient along the road from the river southeast through the Bois de Bavent to Troarn. The perimeter ended just beyond the road junction on the high ground in the Bois de Bavent. Although short of the objective, the salient was important as it was to serve as the jumping-off point for Operation Goodwood forty-three days later.

The 3rd British Division failed to gain its objective that first day as the lead battalions suffered heavy casualties, especially in officers, when they met the German defenders before Caen. The three battalions of the assault brigade suffered 426 casualties. They gained a position roughly three-and-a-half miles from Caen before the stiff resistance of the 21st Panzer Division halted the advance. The 3rd Canadian Division and 50th Division had also penetrated roughly to the same depth but the eastern two divisions had not yet linked-up with the western two.

The British were firmly ashore, and now the requirements were to enlarge the beachhead and bring the full strength and material of the Allies to bear on the German defenders. General Montgomery adjusted his basic battle plan to accommodate the actual situation. His objectives were "to capture Cherbourg and Caen, and develop the central sector of the bridgehead to Caumont and Villers Bocage."[3] Disregarding the American flank, which was peripheral to the battles for Caen, Montgomery's plan was to

---

3. Field Marshal the Viscount Montgomery of Alamein, *Normandy to the Baltic*, p. 86.

launch a series of attacks in either the central area, i.e., around Villers Bocage and Caumont, or from the airborne salient to the east of Caen. By these attacks he was hoping to outflank the German defenders without a frontal assault. This strategy was determined by the strength of the German response to the initial thrust.

Montgomery was also concerned about the supply and reinforcement situation since poor weather conditions slowed the rate at which replacements were arriving. The British had developed an elaborate scheme of supply and maintenance units to support their operations but these required room and time to become fully functional. At no time in the campaign was Montgomery really free from major worries over supplies. Storms, enemy attacks, and the sheer length and complexity of the supply route kept the situation in doubt and occasionally threatened disaster.

The first week after D day was spent in consolidating and organizing the beachhead. When 21st Army Group began its final movements from the beachhead, it was in fact still operating with the divisions that came ashore on D day—the British 7th Armoured, 6th Airborne and the 3rd, 50th and 51st Infantry, and the 3rd Canadian Infantry. The first of the attacks, Operation Perch, was along an axis curving from the area of Balleroy and La Belle Epine southeast to Villers Bocage. The operation, which began on 12 June, was led by the 7th Armoured Division with the 50th Infantry Division on its eastern flank. The armoured column made good progress, and by the morning of the thirteenth the lead battalion of the 7th Armoured Division, the 3rd County of London Yeomanry, had reached and passed through

Villers Bocage. The column consisted of the new British Cromwell tanks in their first combat use and infantry of the 1st Battalion the Rifle Brigade in armoured personnel carriers.

Operation Perch had originally been an elaborate plan that also involved an attack from the airborne salient by 51st Highland Division southwestward behind Caen. When these two hooking arms began to close on the German defenders, an airborne division from Britain then would be dropped into the gap, sealing in the German divisions. The flaw in this carefully designed plan was the strong German resistance and the timely arrival of the 2nd Panzer Division. The 2nd Panzer Division along with a Waffen-SS heavy-tank battalion had been committed by 5th Panzer Army, on the morning of the thirteenth, to occupy the Villers Bocage area.

In the initial contact, the more powerful guns of the Germans were decisive, destroying all the British vehicles that had advanced beyond Villers Bocage. When the Germans penetrated the town, however, they lost the range and power superiority of their guns, and finally both forces rebounded from Villers Bocage. Meanwhile the 50th Division attack just to the left of 7th Armoured Division had met stiff resistance, and, since the 50th was unable to reach the objective of Tilly sur Seulles, 7th Armoured Division was withdrawn to a line roughly from Caumont to Tilly. Fighting continued on the Tilly front until 19 June when the village finally fell.

The eastern attack by the 51st Highland Division also fared badly. The assault was ineptly handled and, as a result of stiff German resistance and severe casualties, the one brigade in action was unable to hold the objective of Saint Honorine la Chardonerette. The 51st Division historian criticized the action thus: "The whole attack seems to a historian to have been hastily arranged, and, as unfortunately is apt so often to happen with the fluid battle, it would appear that in the higher command there was a lack of specific knowledge of the actual situation in and about St. Honorine."[4]

The first offensive had failed by the thirteenth, although fighting continued at Tilly sur Seulles for six more days. On the eighteenth, General Montgomery reiterated, "We must now capture Caen and Cherbourg as the first step in the full development of our plans."[5] He again planned a pincers-type attack with one wing, under the newly arrived VIII Corps, attacking south from midway between Caen and Tilly sur Seulles through Cheux toward Evrecy. Three new divisions had just crossed the Channel and would be used in this attack—the 11th Armoured, 15th Scottish, and 43rd Infantry. The objective would be to capture the area of Bourguebus, Vimont, Bretteville-sur-Laize, i.e., the objective of Operation Goodwood a month later. Initially Montgomery planned to attack from the airborne salient east of the Orne (as Goodwood eventually did), but the area was considered too small to launch an operation of this size. Therefore an exact duplicate of the Perch attack on the left flank occurred, with 51st Highland Division attacking the village of St. Honorine.

This attack, Operation Epsom, was planned for 22

---

4. J. B. Salmond, *The History of the 51st Highland Division 1939–1945*, p. 43.
5. Ellis, *Victory in the West*, p. 271.

June. Before it could be launched, however, a major storm struck the invasion coast. This disturbance forced the British to postpone the attack until, at the earliest, 23 June and in fact until the twenty-sixth. The storm severely damaged the logistical system on the beaches and further delayed the essential build-up of troops. Although the Americans had been doing fairly well in landing reinforcements, the British were two brigades (two-thirds of a division) behind in troop landings at the beginning of the storm and three divisions behind at the end.[6] This delay, of course, applied to all other supplies and thus slowed operations by at least four days, the duration of the storm.

When the storm ended, Epsom was ready to be launched. In addition to the two attacks mentioned, a further assault toward Carpiquet airfield just west of Caen would be carried out in conjunction with Epsom by I Corps with 3rd British and 3rd Canadian Divisions. The major operation (the only one properly called Epsom), that by VIII Corps, began on 26 June and by 29 June had been stopped by heavy German resistance. The attack had carried across the Odon, establishing an important bridgehead, although the troops had not reached Evrecy or threatened the objective area well to the southeast.

The counterattacks against Operation Epsom were the first occasion when elements of the 1st SS Panzer Corps provided the major opposition.

---

6. Ellis, *Victory in the West*, p. 274. This page has detailed figures on this subject. The average number of men landed daily for 21st Army Group dropped from 15,774 to 3,982 during the storm. The Americans dropped behind an equivalent amount.

Mounting the Threat

Throughout this period, all German troop movements, and especially reinforcements from other parts of France, were handicapped by Allied air superiority. In this operation, as in Perch, the British tanks met formidable opposition from the superior German cannon, including conventional artillery, self-propelled guns, and tank armament.[7] Coupled with the heavy armour of German fighting vehicles, superior optics, and the restricted terrain of the beachhead, the German guns enjoyed superiority over Allied armour in this period.

On 23 June, before the rest of Operation Epsom was prepared, 51st Highland Division had carried out its attack, taking and holding St. Honorine against heavy opposition. However, German counterattacks and the limited British reserves prevented any further gains. In the area between the two major thrusts, the I Corps attack never really had a chance. It was predicated on the weakening of German defenses, as the Allies outflanked them to the southwest. But Epsom did not penetrate sufficiently, and the assault was met largely by two new divisions of II SS Panzer Corps drawn from the eastern front rather than by redistribution of the German line. Therefore the weak local attacks were repulsed by strong German defenses in front of Caen. The Epsom salient was strongly counterattacked on 30 June and 1 July, but the Germans did no appreciable damage to the British.

---

7. Appendix D, "Weapon Comparison," gives details, but basically standard German weapons had range and penetration advantages over the Allied equivalents.

Montgomery now planned further operations directed at Caen and at "tidying up" the British front (as he was so fond of doing). He had, at this point, received an additional corps, the XII, and all or part of three more divisions. British losses had mounted to 24,698 men,[8] roughly amounting to two divisions, and American losses were about a third again as large. Montgomery was faced with serious lack of infantry reinforcements for the engaged British units at this point, and this was to become a problem of great importance in the near future.

The next attack was to be launched by the Canadians directly at Carpiquet airfield where the Germans were heavily entrenched. The attackers had the additional problem of the target being a typical airfield—a wide flat area devoid of natural cover or concealment and, after a month's bombardment, of artificial cover. The Canadian attack, Operation Windsor,[9] had been planned for 30 June, but with the failure of Epsom it was postponed until 4 July. A reinforced brigade would attack Carpiquet with massive naval gunfire and air support. The airfield was held by elements of the 12th SS Panzer Division, and when the Canadians attacked behind the massive bombardment, the Germans were able to inflict heavy

---

8. Ellis, *Victory in the West*, p. 307.
9. The narrative on the Canadian attacks, Epsom, and Charnwood is based on Stacey, *The Victory Campaign*. Ellis also covers this period but in less detail. Ross Munro, *Gauntlet to Overlord*; C. P. Stacey, *Canada's Battle in Normandy*; and Kurt Meyer, *Grenadiere* are good from their limited (German or Canadian) viewpoints.

casualties and prevent the Canadians from taking all of the airfield. Although the Germans launched several counterattacks, they were unable to mount one of sufficient strength to push back the Canadians.

Criticism of Montgomery had been building in American circles, over their higher rate of casualties and the apparent lack of success on the British front. Shortly after the Windsor attack, these feelings came to a head in a letter from Eisenhower. The Supreme Commander, in his usual bland manner, alluded to the situation, suggesting more action but not really stating a problem and giving a solution. Montgomery replied that he thought things were going well, and that in fact he was prepared to launch a major attack the next morning aimed at finally capturing Caen north of the Orne.

This operation on 8 July, called Charnwood, the first assault directly against Caen, was to involve a large-scale, high-level bombing attack in its preparation. This attack was originally planned to precede immediately the ground assault but, due to weather problems, was launched the evening before the ground troops attacked. Four hundred sixty-seven bombers of the RAF Bomber Command dropped 2,562 tons of bombs on the targets—the first use of high-level bombing in support of ground troops.[10] The I Corps, under Lieutenant General J. T. Crocker, would make an attack on a three-division front with

---

10. Norman MacMillan, *The Royal Air Force in the World War, Vol. IV*, p. 169. Hilary St. G. Saunders, *Royal Air Force, 1939–45, Vol. III. The Fight is Won*, p. 129, gives 457 aircraft and 2,363 tons of bombs. Stacey, *Victory Campaign*, p. 158, agrees with MacMillan and gives Air Chief Marshal Leigh Mallory, the air commander in chief, as source.

heavy artillery and naval gunfire support in addition to the aerial bombardment. This offensive had been planned just as Epsom ended, and the order issued just as Windsor failed,[11] so slight adjustments became necessary. In any case, after a massive bombardment that caused heavy damage to Caen as well as many civilian casualties, the attackers went in, on the morning of 8 July, to find determined German opposition.

Caen at this time was held by the 12th SS Panzer Division and the 16th Luftwaffe Field Division.[12] The 12th SS were the first line troops under Generalmajor der Waffen-SS Kurt Meyer, an experienced commander. They had been in action since D day but remained effective. The 16th Luftwaffe Field Division was in its first battle and was made up of air force personnel switched with minimal training to an infantry role.

The 59th British Division and the 3rd Canadian Division attacked the center section of Caen, where the SS troops were located. The Panzer division fought well, but by the night of the eighth, the German command withdrew the heavy weapons in support and the next day withdrew virtually all the remaining troops in Caen, in the face of continued

---

11. Stacey, *Victory Campaign*, p. 157-64.
12. 12 SS Panzer Division (Hitler Jugend) has no history per se, but Kurt Meyer, *Grenadiere*, contains a history along with Meyer's other exploits in the war. The only source on the 16th LFD is a manuscript in the U.S. Army *Foreign Military Studies* Series No. B-284, "Die Zerschlagung der 16 Lw. Feld. Div. am 18.7.44 Sudostw. Caen," by General-leutenant Karl Sievers, who was its commander during Operations Charnwood and Goodwood. See also Appendix C, "German Order of Battle.".

British pressure. Because of this action by the Germans, the 12th SS Panzer Division was to fight another day, in Operation Goodwood. The 3rd British Division was in action on the eastern flank, next to the airborne salient, against the positions of the 16th Luftwaffe Field Division.[13] The 16th LFD had suffered heavily in the air attack and, in addition, had the disadvantage of being in action for the first time. One infantry regiment, the 31st Luftwaffe Jaeger Regiment, was severely mauled by the bombers,[14] and consequently the division was quickly pushed back by the D day veterans of the 3rd British Division.

By the afternoon of the ninth, the three assault divisions had cleared Caen north of the Odon. On the tenth, additional attacks on the western edge of I Corps cleared the rest of Carpiquet and brought the British front line up close to the Odon from Caen to the Epsom salient.

Operation Charnwood was to be the predecessor of Goodwood in many ways: the bombardment, the heavy destruction of 16th Luftwaffe Field Division, the lack of real success against first-quality troops with high-level bombing, and the American hostility to British delay.

---

13. British sources use the title "German Air Force Division" (GAF Division), but I feel "Luftwaffe Field Division" (LFD) is more explicit, in addition to being a literal translation of the German title.
14. *Foreign Military Studies.* Mss. B-284 indicates on p. 1329 that 31st Luftwaffe Jaeger Regiment and 16th Luftwaffe Fusilier Battalion were destroyed with the loss of a third of the infantry in the division. Ellis, *Victory in the West*, p. 312, and Stacey, *Victory Campaign*, p. 162, say seventy-five percent of the infantry was lost.

General Montgomery's strategy was slowly being fulfilled: the attacks around Caen were drawing German forces to the British front. The timetable for Overlord had called for capture of Caen by D+5. Since it was D+34, the British were obviously not making the progress they had expected. Montgomery was, however, gaining strength every day. New formations and massive supply stockpiles were in the beachhead; Caen and Cherbourg were in friendly hands. The time had almost arrived for the major attacks that would start the long-expected breakout.

CHAPTER III

Operation Goodwood: The Plan

WITH THE END OF Charnwood, Montgomery had to plan the next stage of his operations to draw the German armour to the British front. The Americans had failed to break out. The initial shock of the invasion, coupled with Hitler's fear of a second invasion, had so far prevented the Germans from mounting a large scale counterattack. But they were beginning to recover. If Hitler's generals could mass a major armoured force, they very possibly could crack a portion of the perimeter. If they could separate the Allies, the Germans might drive them into the sea. It was the concern of all involved that this attack would come on the American front. This conclusion was the result of British conceit, American fear, and German estimates of American inexperience. It was, then, crucially important to keep the German armour committed to the British front. In addition, the British had not yet achieved their goal of the high ground behind Caen, the crucial piece of terrain that was essential to "the threat to Falaise."

Bourguebus Ridge with its commanding heights, open spaces, and road to Falaise and Paris, remained in German hands, and they still had the Orne River as a water barrier along most of their front. These factors allowed the German Armeegruppe West to begin the withdrawal of some of the precious armoured divisions from the British front, in order to position them on the American front. Whether this action was the start of the marshaling of reserves for the dreaded counterattack, or only an attempt to distribute more evenly the available forces for any eventuality, was immaterial; the Allies had to act quickly to preserve the chances of success of their strategy for the liberation of France. And the man who would decide what action to take was the author of that strategy—General Montgomery. Montgomery planned an operation to be called Goodwood after a well-known Sussex racecourse, in keeping with the naming of the previous operations after racecourses in England.[1]

---

1. The name "Goodwood" is in virtually universal use today as the title of this operation. Both Stacey and Ellis use it in their official histories. Contemporary sources, including some documents issued during the battle and collected in *British Army of the Rhine-Battlefield Tour. First Day, 8 Corps Operations East of the Orne, 18–21 July 1944 (Operation Goodwood)*, (Prepared under the direction of G[Trg] HQ British Army of the Rhine, June 1947), use the name "Goodwood Meeting" which is the full name of the race meeting at Goodwood, Sussex.

Operation Goodwood was based on the two major considerations affecting the Allied ground forces in France. The first was the movement of German armour back to the American front. The only positive indication that had been received was the movement of the Panzer Lehr Division from the British front back to the American;[2] but there was great fear that the arrival of infantry divisions from other fronts would lead to the amassing of an armoured force under Panzergruppe West, General der Panzertruppen Freiherr Geyr Von Schweppenburg's headquarters, which was already on the scene.[3] Thus the Second Army had to maintain a threat on its front sufficient to keep the bulk, if not all, of the German armour tied down.

The second major consideration of Operation Goodwood was expansion of the salient. On the Second Army front, the perimeter was still limited and unsatisfactory in many ways. Although Caen had finally fallen at the end of Operation Charnwood, much of the perimeter remained as it had been in mid-June. East of the Orne, from Caen to the sea, the airborne salient remained the same size and shape as it had been after the 51st Division finally captured Saint Honorine la Chardonerette on 23 June. West of the airborne salient, the perimeter followed the Orne through Caen and then along the Odon to the Epsom salient, the small area that the British had captured

---

2. L. F. Ellis, *Victory in the West: Volume I. The Battle of Normandy*, p. 327, that mentions a specific unit movement, although several mention the trend.
3. Alexander McKee, *Caen, the Anvil of Victory*, p. 228, mentions this as do many regimental histories with the exception of Ellis and Stacey.

during Epsom and had managed to retain during heavy counterattacks. The 21st Army Group now held approximately its D day objectives with the exception of the high ground south of the airborne salient and east of Caen—Bourguebus Ridge.

In a conference on 10 July, General Bradley told Montgomery that he was not yet able to break out on the American flank.[4] The fighting on his front had been going too slowly, and his troops were not yet in position for the attack. This made the situation crucial. Montgomery and General Sir Miles Dempsey, his immediate subordinate as Second Army commander, then began to plan Operation Goodwood.

The 21st Army Group had recently received two new divisions: the 11th Armoured Division, which had been in action once, and the Guards Armoured Division, which had not been in action.[5] Also available was the 7th Armoured Division, the "Desert Rats," who had fought through the desert war and had then been the first armoured division to land in Normandy.[6] This force already had been in several actions and was apparently somewhat battle weary in addition to battle experienced. Montgomery and Dempsey decided to group these divisions in an armoured corps, which would be used to strike a single

---

4. Ellis, *Victory in the West*, p. 327; Chester Wilmot, *The Struggle for Europe*, p. 352; B. H. Liddell Hart *The Tanks. Volume II*, p. 359.
5. See *Taurus Pursuant; A History of the 11th Armoured Division* for the 11th, and Captain the Earl Rosse and Colonel E. R. Hill, *The Story of the Guards Armoured Division*, or Major General G. L. Verney, *The Guards Armoured Division*, for the Guards.
6. For this period of the 7th Armoured Division see Major General G. L. Verney, *The Desert Rats* or *History of the 7th Armoured Division, June 1943–July 1945*.

THE LEADERS

Field Marshal the Viscount Montgomery of Alamein, 21st Army Group. At the time of Operation Goodwood, he was still General Sir Bernard Montgomery. As ground forces commander for the Normandy Invasion, Montgomery exercised control over the operations of both the British and American troops in France. His strategy for Goodwood involved using the British to "mount the threat" and keep the Germans occupied while the Americans made the actual breakout.

Lieutenant General Sir Miles C. Dempsey, 2nd British Army. A student at the Staff College under Montgomery, Dempsey had been a corps commander in the desert and Italy and was called back to command Second Army, all under Montgomery. Dempsey's Second Army commanded British ground forces in France and carried out the detailed planning of Goodwood.

Lieutenant General Sir Richard N. O'Connor, 8th Corps. O'Connor had been captured in North Africa and imprisoned in Italy where he escaped after the Italian Armistice. As commander of 8th Corps, he had actual command of the three armoured divisions which made the main thrust of the attack and was responsible for their operational control during the battle.

Major General G.P.B. Roberts with Brigadier C.B.C. Harvey, 11th Armoured Division. Roberts, a Royal Tank Regiment officer, had begun the war as a captain and adjutant of a battalion. After a distinguished career in the desert, Roberts was given command of the 11th Armoured Division in December 1943 at the age of thirty-seven. Regarded by many as Britain's best armour commander, Roberts led the 11th through the rest of the war. Brigadier Harvey commanded 29th Armoured Brigade, the tank element of the 11th. He had also served in the Middle East. The tank in the rear is Harvey's command tank from 29th Brigade.

Major General A.H.S. Adair, Guards Armoured Division. Adair, a Grenadier Guard, commanded a battalion in the British Expeditionary Force in 1940. He then commanded a Guards brigade in Britain and, on the formation of the Guards Armoured Division, one of the two armoured brigades that originally made up that division. In September 1942 he became the division commander and held that post through the rest of the war.

Major General G.W.E.J. Erskine, 7th Armoured Division. Erskine took command of the 7th during the pursuit after El Alamein and led it in Italy. Thus he was the most experienced of the three armoured division commanders.

massive blow from the airborne salient south onto Bourguebus Ridge. This would serve several purposes: it would draw the German armour by providing a massive threat to the vital Falaise area with its access to Paris, thus giving the Americans time to mount their offensive; it would, hopefully, destroy much German armour and personnel by the great weight of the attack; and it would, finally, put the British on Bourguebus Ridge. They would be the captors of all Caen at last, a month after the first attempt.

On 10 July, when Montgomery and Dempsey arrived at the general concept of the operation, they each had a different function or planning task. Montgomery as the army group commander was responsible for overall control; for keeping the Supreme Commander and other high echelons informed; and for liaison, at army group and higher levels, with other supporting forces, in this case the Royal Air Force which was to play a major role. General Sir Miles Dempsey, "Bimbo" as he was known in the army, was the army commander and, as such, was directly responsible for the development of the ground forces plan of action in Goodwood. His planning staff at Second Army was to provide the detailed plan for the operations of VIII Corps and the two flanking corps, I British and II Canadian. The actual plan for the employment of the three armoured divisions would come from VIII Corps planning staff under the corps commander, Lieutenant General Sir Richard N. O'Connor. Much of the later confusion about Operation Goodwood stems from a failure to understand the nature of this command relationship and the exact role of each level of command in planning an operation of this type.

Montgomery, in consultation with Dempsey, arrived at the basic operational plan: to launch a massive attack from the airborne salient toward Bourguebus Ridge, using a corps of three armoured divisions and an extremely heavy bombing attack to prepare the way.[7] This detailed plan was organized and coordinated by Montgomery's headquarters. The army-level plan was based on this, but concerned more basic considerations than the army-group plan, involving supplies, ammunition, artillery, and similar problems. The plans for the three corps involved were even more concerned with details, both of supply and tactics, but with a heavier emphasis on the actual battle and its conduct. Below this level, of course, each division had its own plan, an expansion of the corps plan—just as the corps plan was an expansion of the army plan.

Although it is difficult to trace the exact course of events in the planning of Goodwood, most of the orders survive in some form. Montgomery's concept of the operation is best presented in a document distributed on 15 July to both Dempsey and O'Connor. This paper was titled "Notes on Second Army Operations 16th July–18th July."[8] In this message, Montgomery indicated that the object of Goodwood was "to engage the German armour in battle and 'write it down' to

---

7. Liddell Hart, *The Tanks*, p. 359; G. S. Jackson, *Operations Eighth Corps*, p. 72; and Ellis, *Victory in the West*, p. 327. No source gives any details on this conference.
8. Jackson, *Operations Eighth Corps*, p. 79, and *British Army of the Rhine-Battlefield Tour*, Annex A, contain this document in its entirety. Ellis, *Victory in the West*, pp. 330-31 and C. P. Stacey, *The Victory Campaign*, p. 168, contain abbreviated forms of the message.

such an extent that it would be of no further value to the Germans as a basis of the battle," and "to gain a good bridgehead over the River Orne through Caen and thus to improve our positions on the eastern flank," and finally "generally to destroy German equipment and personnel." He justified this operation in the overall context of the battle for Normandy by writing:

> We require the whole of the Cherbourg and Brittany peninsulas. A victory on the eastern flank will help us to gain what we want on the western flank. But the eastern flank is a bastion on which the whole future of the campaign in North West Europe depends; it must remain a firm bastion; if it became unstable, the operations on the western flank would cease. Therefore, while taking advantage of every opportunity to destroy the enemy, we must be very careful to maintain our own balance and ensure a firm base.[9]

Montgomery then went on to lay out the plan of operations. Under "Initial Operations 8 Corps" he stated, "These three armoured divisions will be required to dominate the area Bourguebus-Vimont-Bretteville, and to fight and destroy the enemy." But he added that "armoured cars should push far to the south towards Falaise and spread alarm and despondency, and discover the form." To emphasize the importance of the crucial Bourguebus Ridge, that is, the

---

9. Jackson, p. 79.

area "Bourguebus-Vimont-Bretteville," Montgomery stated, "while para 5 [Initial Operations 8 Corps] is going on, the Canadians must capture Vaucelles, get through communications and establish themselves in a very firm bridgehead on the general line Fleury-Cormelles-Mondeville." The triangular area between Caen and Bourguebus Ridge was the crucial wedge that tied the armoured objective with the rest of the British front. Montgomery reiterated this in paragraph 7, "Later Operations 8 Corps": "When 6 [Canadian operation] is done, then 8 Corps can 'crack about' as the situation demands. But not before 6 is done." He finished his memorandum with "Finally. Para 6 is vital."[10]

This document clearly sets out the objectives of Goodwood: to capture Bourguebus Ridge and to consolidate a position on that terrain feature. Any further attacks could come only after the main objective was gained by the British and then firmly secured by the Canadians, making a linkup between the ridge and the friendly forces in Caen.

From the moment the initial plan was conceived on the tenth, Montgomery had been busy coordinating and explaining his plan to other services and to his higher headquarters. He had quickly advised Eisenhower of the operation on the tenth,[11] and on the twelfth he sent a modifying telegram indicating that the operation which had originally been planned

10. *Ibid*.
11. Mentioned in Stacey, *Victory Campaign*, p. 167, but not in any other source to my knowledge. Ellis, *Victory in the West*, p. 327, quotes a directive that Montgomery issued on the tenth, but it seems to be to his staff to begin planning.

Operation Goodwood: The Plan / 41

for the fifteenth would be delayed two days. He added that he needed "the whole weight of the air power—to support my land battle, we must have the air to insure success. My whole eastern flank will burst into flames on Saturday and the operation on Monday [the 17th] may have far reaching results.[12] On the thirteenth, Montgomery elaborated in another message, "Am going to launch two very big attacks next week—the big operation on Tuesday 18 July; when 8 Corps with three armoured divisions will be launched to the country east of the Orne." The second big attack that he mentioned was the U.S. First Army attack west of St. Lo. He emphasized, "The whole weight of air power will be required for Second Army on 18 July and First Army on 19th July."[13] By the time this message was sent, Operation Goodwood had been delayed another day because of weather conditions and the need to reorganize the participating units.

On the fourteenth, Montgomery informed the Chief of the Imperial General Staff and the Director of Military Operations[14] of his plans. In these messages he emphasized the immense possibilities that a breakthrough or heavy destruction of the Germans would present.[15] He also had to indicate the need for

---

12. Stacey, *Victory Campaign*, p. 167.
13. Stacey, *Victory Campaign*, p. 167; Ellis, *Victory in the West*, p. 328. There are considerable differences in the texts of the two quotes. I used Stacey's version since it seems more complete.
14. These were Montgomery's British superiors as opposed to his Allied superiors: the men to whom he was responsible for his use of the British units in his command.
15. Ellis, *Victory in the West*, pp. 329-30.

caution, however, especially since the Second Army was the only British force available to carry the banner of Great Britain in the liberation of Europe. An overly enthusiastic attack might well lead to the defeat in detail of the overextended British.

With the final message of the fifteenth to Dempsey and the corps commanders, Montgomery's role actually became rather secondary, as the operation itself was really in the hands of the army and corps commanders. Dempsey already had his staff working on the plans, of course; and on the seventeenth he issued his order entitled "Second Army Operations; commencing on 18th July."[16] This order was divided into two portions according to the natural division of his front. West of the Orne, XII Corps and XXX Corps were to make demonstrations to their front to draw the maximum German forces away from the zone east of the Orne where the main attack was to be launched. Dempsey had three corps: I and VIII British and II Canadian. First Corps would only make a limited attack on the east edge of the airborne salient. The 3rd British Division, the unit that was to have captured Caen on D day, would attack southeast to the area of Sannerville and Troarn, covering the left flank of the armoured divisions. Second Canadian Corps on the other flank would capture and hold Vaucelles, the industrial suburb of Caen on the south bank of the Orne, and then, on order, advance to Fleury and Cormelles to secure the right flank as the battle progressed.

---

16. Jackson, *Operation Eighth Corps*, p. 81; *British Army of the Rhine-Battlefield Tour*, Annex B. Liddell Hart, *The Tanks*, mentions this order (pp. 360-61), but the other secondary sources ignore it.

In the center, VIII Corps had the main task. It would "establish armoured divisions in the area; (a) Vimont, (b) Garcelles-Secqueville, (c) Hubert Folie-Verrieres," that is, on Bourguebus Ridge. "The task of these three divisions will be to get their main bodies so established that there can be no enemy penetration through the ring," and, of course, the normal tasks of destroying the defenders and repelling any counterattacks that might be launched at them. In keeping with British army doctrine and good military sense, patrolling and exploitation would be carried out to the south toward Falaise, within the limits of the Dives on the east and the Orne on the west. But, in keeping with his commander's caution about overextending, Dempsey stated: "Main bodies of the three divisions will not be moved from areas (a), (b), (c) [Bourguebus Ridge], without reference to me."[17]

The scheme of maneuver for Operation Goodwood had now been formulated and passed down to corps level. It was to be a central armoured stroke to capture Bourguebus Ridge with secondary attacks to secure the flanks of the main thrust and also to take advantage of the confusion produced by the attack. There was only one more army-group and army-level consideration to be dealt with—fire support. For Goodwood this fire support took two forms: a massive aerial bombardment to prepare the area for the attack by destroying the majority of German fortifications, and a heavy artillery barrage just before and during the attack to neutralize specific targets and deal with any unreduced strong points. The aerial bombardment was to cause the most difficulty since it

---

17. Jackson, *Operation Eighth Corps*, p. 81.

required interservice cooperation. Many of the messages Montgomery sent to Eisenhower about the importance of this attack were probably attempts to gain support for the use of aircraft, for there was considerable difficulty in getting the necessary amount of support.

In any case, sufficient air support was forthcoming, and a detailed plan for the use of air support evolved.[18] The initial air attack would be from 0545 to 0630 hours and would involve 1,056 heavy night bombers of the Royal Air Force. This assault would be directed at the flanks of the Goodwood area, in lines along the Caen suburbs on the west and Sannerville, Banneville, and Cagny on the east. The bombings were to be with high-explosive ordnance and were designed to knock out any German position that could rake the exposed flanks of the divisions.

The next wave of the air assault would be at 0700 and last another forty-five minutes. The target would be the central area including the villages of Cuverville, Demouville, and Giberville. The attack would be carried out by 482 medium bombers of the 9th U.S. Army Air Force, using only fragmentation bombs. In this case, the idea was to destroy the enemy and his weapons without heavily cratering the area through which the tanks would have to pass. The third bombing attack would be similar, involving 539 heavy day bombers, again American, in attacks on the villages in

---

18. Jackson, *Operation Eighth Corps*, p. 89; *British Army of the Rhine-Battlefield Tour*, p. 28. Both have basically the same information which is the most complete. All the general sources also have some limited details. The two RAF books, MacMillan and Saunders, have only the briefest details.

the final objective area on the ridge. This attack would begin at 0830, after the armoured divisions had begun to roll forward, and last a half hour. There would also be scattered bombing throughout the area and additional heavy bombing beyond the ridge to deal with the German artillery in that area.

The artillery fire plan was equally complex.[19] A total of 760 guns was to be used, belonging to thirty-seven different units drawn not only from the attacking divisions but from virtually every formation in the area. Because of the confined area of the salient, no guns could be deployed in that zone; therefore, many targets that could have been engaged by artillery were left strictly to the air forces. This decision especially applied to the ridge itself and was to cause unfortunate results. Two monitors and a cruiser of the Royal Navy were also included in the plan, assigned to engage coastal guns to the east and north of the salient at Franceville and Cabourg.

For the 456 field guns involved in Goodwood, there were 500 rounds each; for the medium artillery, 208 in number, there were 300 rounds each; and for the 96 heavy guns, only 150 rounds.[20] This ammunition was to be used in a five-phase attack. Phase I

---

19. *British Army of the Rhine-Battlefield Tour*, p. 23 and 97-8, and Jackson, *Operation Eighth Corps*, p. 86, must be taken together for a detailed view. Other sources are weak. See T. J. Bell, *Into Action with the Twelfth Field*, W. Brownlie Steele, *The Proud Trooper*, and *25th Field Regiment, Royal Artillery, Northwest Europe 1944-1945* for units involved.
20. In the British service, "field" means the 25 pounder (87.6mm), "medium" is the 4.5- or 5.5-inch, and "heavy" is the 155mm gun or 7.2-inch howitzer, or in this case also the 3.7-inch heavy anti-aircraft gun.

would be an attempt to maintain normal appearances with only anti-flak counterbattery fire. This deception would be maintained up to and during the bombing. In phase II, from H-100 to H-10,[21] all guns would fire counterbattery against the German artillery in the area. At H hour, phase III would begin with eight field regiments, the most rapid-firing guns, firing on a front of 2,000 yards, in front of the advancing units. This rolling barrage would advance at a rate of 150 yards-a-minute to a depth of 4,300 yards to allow for the advance of the divisions, while the rest of the artillery fired concentrations on the flanks to neutralize known or suspected enemy positions. At H+80 the field regiments would revert to their divisions, and each division would have on call a portion of the corps artillery. This fourth phase would end at H+200. Each division then would have only one additional medium regiment on call during the fifth phase which would include the rest of the operation.[22]

In this manner Dempsey tried to maintain maximum artillery support for his men, although the size of the salient was a great handicap. Both the air and artillery attacks were designed to afford optimum protection to the ground forces. The barrages would clear the way ahead of the advancing troops while screening the attackers from the sides as well.

General Montgomery, General Dempsey and their staffs had now done virtually everything they

---

21. H hour is the hour that the lead element should cross the start line of an operation; for Goodwood it was 0745.
22. This detailed breakdown appears on page 23 of the *BAOR Battlefield Tour*. No other source approaches this detail but none contradicts it.

could for Operation Goodwood. They had worked out a reasonably clever overall plan: a massive blow by three armoured divisions from the least-likely spot, preceded by a heavy air bombardment. They had planned a heavy artillery barrage and coordinated naval gunfire and air support. It was now up to the troop leaders to plan for their own operations and prepare their units for the attack on Bourguebus Ridge.

CHAPTER IV

The Opposing Forces

WITH THE PLAN complete, 21st Army Group now needed some of the finest regiments of Britain to make this great charge. To conduct an operation of this size, every type of unit in the British army would be required, both combat and support, but armoured units would of course provide the most important activity.

Britain had developed the tank, and much of the early doctrine of armoured warfare had been evolved by their military intellectuals. But Britain had not always been a nation to heed its prophets; and it also had gone through a great depression just at the crucial time for pre-war rearmament. These factors left Britain with a second-rate armoured force at the beginning of the Second World War. In the early campaigns the British army had only been able to field a very small armoured force with inadequate vehicles and a tactical doctrine keyed to the use of tanks solely in a support role for infantry units. This doctrine, along with the majority of the early tanks, was left at Dunkirk. Fortunately, the British armoured forces soon began to rebound.

Much of the experienced personnel and better equipment had gone to the Middle East before the war, and from this nucleus grew a successful mechanized army. Initially with second-rate British equipment and later with modern American lend-lease vehicles, the armoured formations of the Eighth Army fought a magnificent armoured war. With the open spaces of North Africa and with largely mechanized forces on both the English and German sides, the type of operation envisaged by many of the early writers on mechanized warfare existed. Vast tank fleets ranged across the desert or hid behind minefields in small defended harbours. The infantry fought set-piece battles and defended fixed locations, but the decisive maneuvers were mechanized. The British army and the British people enjoyed ascendancy over the Axis powers during three years of this classic armoured warfare. Mastery of this type of warfare coupled with the supply capabilities of the American tank arsenals won the day for Britain in North Africa.

The next field of battle was Italy and unfortunately that sunny country is mountainous. The Germans depended on the natural fortifications and based their defenses on the inaccessible mountains. Because of these tactics, the three Commonwealth armoured divisions committed in Italy had little opportunity to change the ideas that had developed in desert warfare. Italy was regarded as a unique situation, and any lessons learned there were not considered to affect normal armoured operations. Thus the three armoured divisions in England, two new and one desert veteran, had little recent experience on which to base their Normandy doctrine.

The Germans had been in heavy ground combat, over all types of terrain, against a variety of foes but primarily the Russians. The Russians employed large numbers of tanks as well as huge masses of people, which affected their tactics. They tended to use large-scale attacks with heavy armour support. This experience influenced German tactics, which favored mobile defenses in depth with small battle groups of tanks and infantry, and maximum anti-tank weapon support. These groups were often placed in small villages or farms to form a series of interlocking strongpoints. It was to be these two doctrines of warfare that clashed on Bourguebus Ridge.

In the summer of 1944, the British armoured division had reached the apex of its development. It had gone through several major and many minor changes in the early years of the war, but after the first few months of 1944 the divisional organization remained the same for the rest of the war except for various equipment changes. The division was divided into two basic components, an armoured brigade and an infantry brigade; each of these two main fighting elements was commanded by a brigadier.[1] The normal composition of an armoured brigade was three

---

1. Brigadier is the British rank equivalent to brigadier-general in most armies; however, in Britain he normally commands units of one type only and thus is not considered a general officer.

armoured regiments[2] of seventy-two tanks each, and a motor battalion. The motor battalion was 819 infantry men especially equipped with either light trucks or half-tracks and trained in close cooperation with armoured formations. This armoured brigade was the senior one in the division and was normally commanded by the senior (i.e., most experienced) brigadier. The infantry brigade consisted of three standard infantry battalions which, unlike the motor battalion, were without special training, except as the division had provided, and were without armoured vehicles. In other words, it was basically a normal infantry brigade which happened to be in an armoured division. This lack of mobility, of course, greatly decreased its ability to help the armoured brigade in many situations. The division also contained two battalions of field artillery (twenty-four guns each), one of which was mounted on self-propelled carriages; an anti-tank regiment, half towed and half self-propelled, of twenty-four 17-pounders; an anti-aircraft regiment; an armoured reconnaissance regiment; and a variety of general support troops. The armoured reconnaissance regiment was a normal armoured regiment in strength but was equipped with

---

2. Unit nomenclature in Britain is somewhat confused. In armoured and cavalry usage, regiment is the title of the basic battalion-sized formation, while in the infantry, regiment is a nebulous parent organization which may contain any number of battalions. A further confusion to Americans may be that while squadron is equal to battalion and troop to company in the United States army, in the British army, squadron is a company within the regiment and troop is a platoon, basically used only in armoured and cavalry units, but also in some engineer and artillery units.

fast tanks and trained for reconnaissance missions rather than a main battle role. The general support troops included a venerable British anachronism left from the First World War—the machine gun company. In all, the armoured division consisted of 14,964 men with 3,414 vehicles of which 290 were tanks.[3]

The armoured divisions had been equipped with a variety of tanks during the war, the majority of which had, or have since developed, bad reputations in comparison with the equipment of the Germans.[4] In 1944 there were two standard cruisers or main battle tanks[5] in the British army—the American Sherman and the British Cromwell. The Sherman had been a lend-lease item since its inception and was available in great quantities. It was an unspectacular but successful design, normally armed with a 75mm gun which had limited effectiveness against the heavily armoured German tanks, although it was by no means helpless against them. The Sherman served as the basic tank of the armoured regiments of the Guards and 11th Armoured Division in Operation Goodwood.

---

3. All details in this discussion are taken from L. F. Ellis, *Victory in the West, Vol. 1, The Battle of Normandy* pp. 533-40. They also appeared in J. F. Joslen, *Orders of Battle, Second World War, Vol. I* pp. 9-10.
4. See Appendix D, "Weapon Comparison."
5. The term "cruiser tank" in the British service was used to distinguish those tanks that were to cruise the battlefield and do combat with the enemy's tanks; the cruiser was the main battle tank. The "infantry tank," which was more heavily armoured and slower, was found in the tank brigade that supported infantry divisions.

The British-designed and built Cromwell was a much more spectacular vehicle than the Sherman. It was fast for a tank and had a lower profile, a distinct advantage in combat. With a Christie (high speed) type of suspension, the Cromwell even looked like a fast tank, like a breakthrough or cavalry type, beloved of the armour advocates who believed in the tank as the ultimate weapon. Primarily as a result of the inability of the British tank industry to produce great numbers of vehicles, there were not enough Cromwells to equip all British armoured formations; so only the senior armoured division, the 7th, was totally equipped with these vehicles. Only the armoured reconnaissance regiments of the other divisions, who could, in theory at least, use the speed of the Cromwell in their missions, were equipped with this tank. Aside from the greater speed of the Cromwell, however, there was little difference between it and the Sherman, as they were armed with the same cannon and had roughly the same degree of armoured protection. The armour was adequate against medium-caliber weapons including the 75mm cannon, but it did not stand up well against the heavy-caliber guns that the Germans were using at this time. It should be noted that the German armour was equally vulnerable to the British heavy anti-tank weapons.

The Germans, in a defensive role and haunted by the spectre of their Russian experience, emphasized heavy guns and, because they were on the defensive, were able to employ the heavy and cumbersome weapons. The British recognized the problem, and their solution was to augment the firepower of the

THE WEAPONS

Cromwell tanks of the 2nd (Armoured Reconnaissance) Battalion, The Welsh Guards, at Escoville on July 18. The Cromwell, the most modern British tank, equipped all of the 7th Armoured Division and the armoured reconnaissance battalions of the other two divisions. Armed with a 75mm gun, Cromwell units had to be reinforced with 17-pounder-equipped Shermans to defend against the latest German tanks.

Sherman tank advancing past a German Pz. Mark IV tank near Cagny. The American Sherman, provided under lend-lease, formed the backbone of British armoured divisions. The armoured battalions in the 11th and Guards Armoured Divisions were equipped with Shermans. Reliability and availability, rather than performance, were the Sherman's strong points. The Mark IV was the standard German medium tank at this period. The example, presumably of 21st Panzer Division which occupied the Cagny area, is equipped with supplemental armour to protect against shaped-charge anti-tank weapons.

Sherman Firefly. Because the standard 75mm gun in the Sherman performed inadequately against German tanks, the British began a program of producing modified tanks with the 17-pounder anti-tank gun mounted. This gun had substantially improved penetration but was easily detected and became a priority target for German gunners. One Firefly was assigned to each troop in armoured battalions, making up about twenty percent of the tank strength.

Tiger and Panther tanks. The Tiger I, armed with an 88mm gun, equipped two companies of the 503rd SS Heavy Tank Battalion near Cagny. The heavily armoured Tigers were badly damaged by the bombing, and the survivors were destroyed in combat with the armoured divisions. A Panther, the medium tank which formed part of 21st Panzer Division, is visible in the background.

armoured units on the following basis. One of every four vehicles was a more heavily gunned Sherman or, in rare cases, an up-gunned Cromwell. The up-gunned Sherman was the "Firefly," with a modified seventeen-pound anti-tank gun mounted in a slightly redesigned turret. The seventeen-pounder, which also equipped the anti-tank regiment of the division, was superior in range and armour penetration to the fabled German 88 gun but was obvious to enemy observers in battle because of its greater barrel length. Thus the Firefly had a short combat life on the battlefield. But in the brief period before the Germans were able to knock out the Fireflys, they were capable of dealing with anything the Germans could offer.

The British armoured divisions also contained a third type of tank, the "Honey." This was an American M3 or M5 light tank—a small, lightly armoured and very out-dated vehicle with a 37mm gun. Eleven of these outmoded vehicles were in a reconnaissance troop at each armoured regiment headquarters and were used for scouting and screening tasks. These tanks were no match for any modern fighting vehicle; in fact, the British were so contemptuous of the puny armament that they often removed the entire turret, feeling that a low profile offered better protection than the main gun. None the less, the Honey made up fifteen percent of the numerical strength in tanks of the regiment and thus the division.

The British had four combat-ready armoured divisions in 1944. One of these, the 6th, was in Italy where in the rugged terrain it could do little more than support infantry assaults by fire. The remaining three were in Normandy and would be used in Operation Goodwood. One was among the most experienced divisions in the British army, having been in the desert since 1938. The others were new and untried: one was made up of largely temporary war-created units; the other had been organized, in a flurry of controversy, from the regiments of Foot Guards. The different backgrounds of these divisions were to have varying effects on their performance in this operation.

The 7th Armoured Division proudly wore the red jerboa (desert rat) formation sign, proclaiming them as the famous unit that had formed the armoured backbone of Britain's victorious desert army. The battalions of this division had been among the first to form a major armoured formation, and they had a tradition of fierce support of armoured warfare, born in the days when it was not fashionable to be in armour. This first British armoured formation of divisional size had been the Mobile Division, formed in Egypt in 1938.[6] It had been in the forefront of each North African campaign, alternately either defeating the Italians and Germans or being nearly destroyed itself. After the end of the desert campaign, the 7th served briefly in Italy, landing at Salerno.[7] It had then been withdrawn to prepare for the invasion of northwestern Europe.

The 7th Armoured Division arrived in England on 7 January 1944 and trained until its embarkation

---

6. B. H. Liddell Hart, *The Tanks, Vol. II*, p. 36.
7. *History of 7th Armoured Division June 1943–July 1945*, p. 4-20.

for Normandy. During this period the composition and command of the division remained virtually the same as it had been throughout the last of the desert campaign and during the Italian operations. These men were very experienced but were also tired, having been in a great deal of combat.

The division landed in Normandy on D+1, 7 June 1944, and was the only armoured division in the beachhead for the first two weeks. As such, Montgomery used it to lead several of the early attacks on the western edge of the British front (detailed in Chapter I). The division had not done well in this early fighting and several subordinate commanders had been removed by the division commander, Major General G.W.E.J. Erskine.[8] Command problems were to continue through Goodwood and were probably the result of officers becoming overly cautious and weary after years of combat.

The 11th Armoured Division was completely different from its older sister. One of the large number of new armoured divisions which had been formed in the initial burst of mobilization after the first German successes, it had spent the intervening time training in England. Many of its units were also wartime creations, units without the traditions and esprit de corps of the regular regiments but also without the prejudices and conservatism of tradition. There were many experienced men throughout the ranks and a better-than-average commander in G.P.B. Roberts.

---

8. Conversation with Major General G.P.B. Roberts and others, at Cabourg, Calvados, 7 June 1971. These events are not mentioned in any history.

"Pip" Roberts was one of a new breed of regular officers, having been commissioned into the Royal Tank Corps in 1926. He had thus received a great deal of experience in armoured tactics and had participated in many of the training debates of the 1930s. Roberts had served the entire war in armoured units and had risen from battalion adjutant to brigade commander in the 7th Armoured Division in four years campaigning in the desert.[9] Many of his subordinates had also served in the desert. Thus a fairly good experience level existed in the higher echelons, while the bulk of the personnel was fresh although highly trained.

The Guards Armoured Division differed from both of the above divisions. The last of the three to be organized, its creation was controversial. Many people opposed the idea of a Guards Division because it would place all of the presumably highly trained troops of the Brigade of Guards in one formation rather than distributing them and their skills throughout the army. Secondly, it would require an unnecessarily large training effort to turn out the number of Guards replacements which could be expected for a division in combat. And finally, many wondered if the Guards could adjust to serving in an armoured unit, since the qualities and values required were not the same as those needed to mount successfully a King's Guard at Buckingham Palace or otherwise to survive in an extremely fashionable unit. However, the Guards Armoured Division was

---

9. *Battlefield Tour: Operation Goodwood*, p. 9. Pamphlet prepared by the Staff College, Camberley, for participants in the tour of Bourguebus Ridge.

formed, and the men had attained a fairly high degree of skill by the time they were called on to undertake their first combat service. Because there were no other Guards armoured formations, few of their officers had any combat experience in tanks, although many probably had more experience with motor vehicles than the average Englishman, as between the wars cars were still luxury items in England. Since the Guards Division had to be commanded by a Guards officer, it would be an individual with little armoured experience. Major General A.H.S. Adair was the officer chosen, and he was to prove an extremely able and innovative commander. Perhaps as a result of being the last armoured division organized, this division was the last to arrive in Normandy where it deployed shortly before Operation Goodwood. Only the Guards infantry brigade was employed before Goodwood and then only briefly in a defensive position.

These British armoured divisions had been trained in the tactical concepts of their army—concepts that had evolved up to the end of the North African campaign the previous year. These tactics emphasized the idea of tanks in armoured divisions as the main striking force to fight enemy tanks and to exploit breakthroughs. While other formations were designed to support infantry units, the armoured division was a monolithic force designed to capture large areas and carry out large-scale movements. The armoured brigade was the main striking force in this concept. It penetrated the enemy defenses and gained ground. The infantry brigade would then follow, clearing pockets of resistance and defending the gains. If the tanks were held up, then the mission of the infantry would be to restore the mobility of the armoured units by conducting standard infantry attacks, supported by the tanks. Once the obstacle was overcome, the armour would resume the lead. Other units would deal with detailed defenses and secure captured terrain.

This had been a viable technique in the desert where there were vast areas to be dealt with and large enemy armoured forces to fight. However, in the relatively close quarters of Normandy (although admittedly not as confined as the Bocage would be later) this lack of regard for close coordination with infantry was to be a severe handicap.[10] Later in the campaign this was recognized, and task groups based on much closer cooperation were used.

The basic employment of the division was based on the tactical concept described above. The armoured reconnaissance regiment would be employed as a screening or flanking force. In this role it could most effectively use the speed of its Cromwell tanks and, since this would be strictly an armoured operation, the army had not felt it necessary to train this regiment to fight with infantry. This idea was part of the classic concept of tank warfare: screen the flanks with a thin line of fast tanks while thrusting with the main force.

The armoured brigade of a division would make the main thrust, followed by the infantry brigade to mop up survivors and secure the terrain. This main thrust would normally take the form of a two-battalion front with the third battalion in reserve, if

---

10. General Roberts; Liddell Hart, *The Tanks*, p. 364.

space permitted, which it did not in the early stages of Goodwood. This "two up, one back" system was standard throughout the British army: in the battalions two companies or squadrons would be up and one back, and two platoons up and one back; and within armoured formations this would apply even to the troop of three or four tanks where there would normally be a two-tank front with the remaining vehicles to the rear. This policy, of course, could be and frequently was modified to accommodate special situations.

This formation would be used for movement and for attacking lightly held or unknown positions. In the case of strong points or heavy weapons, the reserve element and/or one of the lead elements would form a base of fire and the remaining elements would attempt to flank the target. This last tactic was much used by the weakly armed and armoured Shermans in trying to deal with the German 88s, both field and tank guns. One of the great problems in Goodwood was that the clear fields of fire allowed for little of this type of maneuver against the German defenses.

The German defenses were manned by a variety of units, all of which had been manhandled to some degree in the month since D day. These units were understrength and in some cases severely demoralized from previous battles and long commitment to the front. Their equipment similarly suffered from the effects of the defeats that had brought them to their present positions. However, the majority of the German commanders had extensive experience in mobile defenses having fought in Russia and/or North Africa, and the better-quality troops found in army and Waffen SS armoured formations were still very efficient.

Starting with the left flank of the British salient, the first German unit was the 346th Infantry Division, one of the coastal defense divisions that had been on the coast since before D day and, although not a first-line division, had conducted a satisfactory defense. Across the front of the salient (where three armoured divisions would soon be attacking) lay the remnants of the 16th Luftwaffe Field Division. This unit, which had just lost a third of its strength in Caen as a result of Operation Charnwood,[11] had received virtually no reinforcements and had very low morale. At the right end of the salient lay the 272nd Infantry Division, a unit which had been destroyed once before and subsequently reconstituted.[12] It was just arriving in the line to relieve the 1st SS Panzer Division and so was the freshest of the German formations in this area. The 1st SS Panzer Division remained in the area just behind its former position and occupied the western end of Bourguebus Ridge and the reverse slope.[13] On the forward slope, occupying the space between the front line and crest, was the 21st Panzer Division. This division had barred the way to Caen on D day and had been used since then as a mobile reserve on this sector of the front. Their troops were worn but not by any means defeated or demoralized. Because

---

11. See Chapter 2, p. 37.
12. Martin Jenner, *Die 216/272 niedersachsische Infanterie-Division 1938–1945*.
13. German positions remain difficult to locate precisely. My order of battle is based on G. S. Jackson, *Operations Eighth Corps*, p. 69, and *Battlefield Tour* pamphlet, p. 7, 8, and 19.

The Opposing Forces / 63

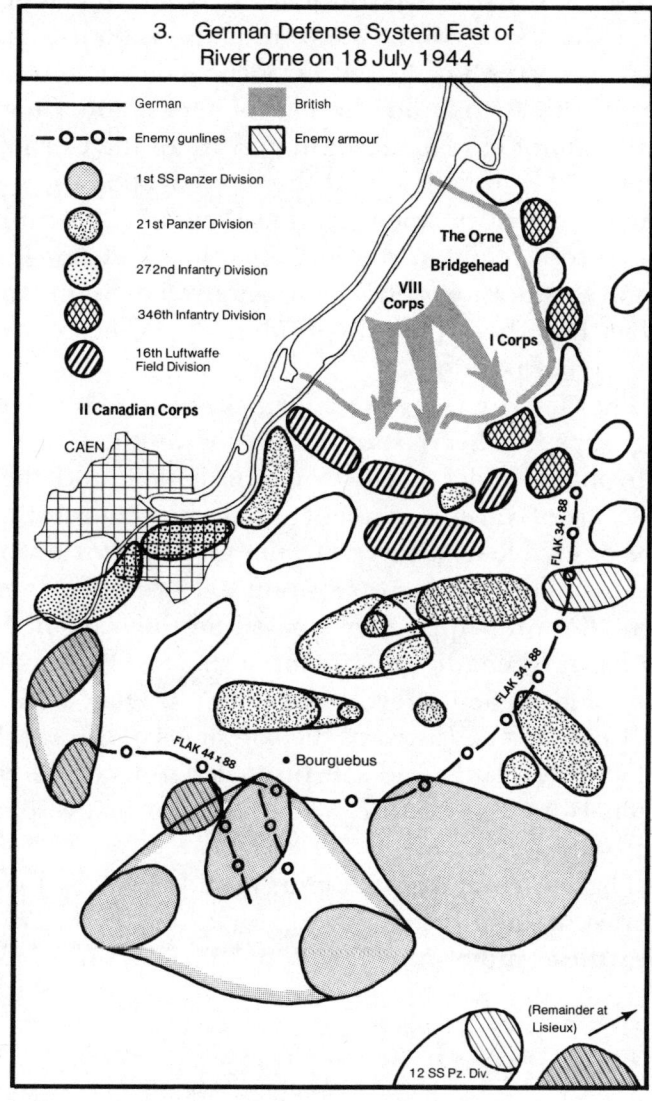

of the heavy casualties and the confusion of this period, it is extremely difficult to determine much about the exact composition and disposition of the German forces facing the airborne salient; and, of course, the British on the eve of Operation Goodwood did not have an accurate picture of the German situation. From patrols and the interrogation of prisoners, the British knew the locations of these units that were actually in the line, but they had no clear idea of the location of the two armoured divisions and in fact had them placed considerably to the rear of their actual positions.[14]

The German units were normally divided into battle groups for this type of defense in depth. The battle group would be based on a unit staff and then made up of various elements of that unit and other units to enable it to carry out the mission. For example, the main German opposition to Goodwood came from "Kampfgruppe Luck" based on the staff of the 125 Panzergrenadier Regiment of the 21st Panzer Division and named after its commander, Oberst Hans von Luck.[15] It consisted of the battalions of the 125th, and attached tanks and self-propelled guns of the division. During the battle, von Luck also made some impromptu attachments.

These various German units would normally form a series of interlocking strongpoints in depth. As a rule they utilized villages or farms for these

---

14. Jackson, p. 72; *Battlefield Tour* pamphlet, p. 7, 8.
15. Talk by Oberst a.D. Hans von Luck at the 1971 Battlefield Tour, June 7, 1971 near Cabourg, Calvados. Von Luck is a regular participant in these tours and his role loses nothing from year to year.

strongpoints, taking advantage of the strong stone walls of the Norman buildings for added protection. This defense in depth covered the entire area from the front line to the crest of the ridge. Along or just behind the crest lay a line of about eighty 88mm guns which were intended to be part of the defenses of Caen.[16] Thus the British, poised to assault the ridge, faced an extremely hostile landscape, with virtually every group of buildings a strongpoint and Germans almost as far as the eye could see.

As the last phase of preparation for Operation Goodwood began, two very different armies faced each other. The British had a massive tank army, designed to attack and destroy other such armies and then exploit the breakthrough. The troops were well equipped but with somewhat vulnerable equipment. Opposing them was a battered army, experienced in defense against the type of attack the British would make, positioned on favorable terrain, and having had adequate time to prepare for its defense. The Germans were, however, handicapped by their previous losses, by combat fatigue, and by the great quantitative, if not qualitative, superiority of the attackers.

---

16. The location and intended use of these weapons is a source of considerable controversy. Most sources indicate an extensive gun line along the ridge which did considerable damage. Von Luck says that there was one battalion of anti-aircraft 88mm guns and one battalion of self-propelled anti-tank weapons behind the ridge and that the commander of the 21st, being an old artillery officer, would not commit them because of fear of losing them.

CHAPTER V

The Battle: First Day

ONCE THE ARMY PLAN for Operation Goodwood was complete and the divisions had received the basic order, it was the responsibility of the corps commander to plan the exact operation his units would carry out. It had been established in the 21st Army Group order that 11th Armoured Division would be the lead division in the assault, so General O'Connor and his staff had to plan the detailed scheme of maneuver that each element of his corps would follow. Each division commander—Roberts of the 11th, Erskine of the 7th, and Adair of the Guards—was also planning the movement of his troops, but since the 11th was the lead division the other two would have to conform to its movements.

Of course, the corps itself was restricted, by the duration and location of the preparatory barrage, in what it could do and when it could start. In addition, none of the assaulting divisions were in or near the airborne salient from which the attack would be launched, and the salient could hold only one division. An elaborate plan was required to move that one division into the salient without alerting the Germans and also to provide for the movement of the two following divisions through the salient at the height of the battle. This was especially important since there existed only a limited number of roads into and through the salient, and only three bridges that could carry tanks across the water barriers at the base of the salient, the Orne and the Canal de Caen.

The basic scheme of maneuver for the three armoured divisions was created by General O'Connor's staff at VIII Corps Headquarters and then passed on to the three division commanders. To understand this plan it is necessary to be familiar with the terrain of the area in which the attack would be launched.

Looking from the airborne salient to the objective, the observer is struck by an impression of a vast open plain dipping to a low crease in the center and then rising to a low ridge in the background. Knowing the fame of Bourguebus Ridge, one's greatest impression is of how low the ridge actually is; it is a low, gently rolling elevation which, from the location of General Robert's headquarters just west of Amfreville, seems to be the slightest of inclines. The entire plain is open agricultural land, cultivated primarily for field crops, with occasional clumps of trees through which one or two roofs are visible, marking the small villages which lie on the plain.[1]

The villages can be classified into three groups: the intermediate, lying on the plain between the airborne salient and the ridge; the ridge villages, which were the objectives; and the peripheral villages on either side of the main avenue of advance. From the Goodwood start line, the first villages are Cuverville and Demouville, which lie just to the left of the main axis of advance and in line with it. On either side are peripheral villages, Colombelles and Giberville on the west and Touffreville, Sannerville, Banneville, and Emieville on the east. Thus the first part of the Goodwood attack was through a funnel of small villages that flanked the Allied armour, although these villages, of course, were to be neutralized before H hour by the bombardment.

Beyond this first group of villages there is a second group where the Caen-Vimont road cuts across the plain. Listed in order of proximity to Caen, le Mesnil Frementel and Cagny are situated on the north side of the road, and Grentheville, le Poirier, Frenouville, and Vimont are to the south. These villages, the first objectives, were located in the area where the aerial bombardment would weaken in intensity. Between the Vimont road and the Falaise road is another group of villages—Bras, Soliers,

---

1. This description is based on study of 1:25,000 scale maps, 1:200,000 scale maps, the author's visit to the area, and photographs taken during that visit.

Hubert Folie, Four, Bourguebus, la Hogue, Tilly-la-Campagne, Secqueville, Garcelles, and Cramesnil—which forms a hedgehog pattern and provides the best defensive positions in the plain. Beyond the Falaise road are the villages with which Goodwood was concerned—Ifs, Verrieres, and Rocquancourt.

The only significant obstacle to troop movements on this plain is an embanked railway line running from Colombelles due south to the vicinity of Bourguebus and thus directly across the line of advance of 11th Armoured Division from le Mesnil Frementel to Hubert Folie. The grade of the embankment is about twenty feet above the general terrain. There are gaps at intervals where various roads pass through, but a two-lane road under the railway line simply formed a choke point for the movement of tanks and channeled the 29th Armoured Brigade into a bottleneck just as it reached the final objectives.

The commanding generals were, to some extent, unhappy with the extremely detailed orders that came down to them from Headquarters, VIII Corps. These orders directed that certain units perform specified tasks in the assault. As the terrain over which they would be moving was difficult, these movement requirements would place a severe strain on the troops. The division commanders, although seriously distressed, were able to overcome the difficulties and arrange their divisions for the tasks. The VIII Corps attack was launched on schedule, and the troops of the three divisions were able to arrive at the start line in time.

The orders received by 11th Armoured Division precisely assigned the tasks.[2] In the first phase of the operation, the 3rd Royal Tank Regiment[3] would lead through the gap in the minefield surrounding the friendly perimeter and proceed for 2,500 yards beyond (roughly to the vicinity of Cuverville). Then another armoured regiment of the 29th Armoured Brigade, the Second Fife and Forfar Yeomanry,[4] would move alongside the 3rd RTR on the left as the minefields were passed, and the advance would continue on a two-battalion front toward the first objective, the small village of le Mesnil Frementel. This village would be occupied by the motor battalion of the 29th Armoured Brigade which was the 8th Rifle Brigade.[5] If Cagny, just to the northeast of le Mesnil Frementel, was occupied, it would be "watched and neutralized"[6] until the follow-up division, the Guards Armoured Division, arrived on the scene.

The infantry brigade of the 11th Division, the 159th, was to cross the start line at the same time as

---

2. These tasks are listed in *British Army of the Rhine—Battlefield Tour*, p. 13, and in *Battlefield Tour: Operation Goodwood* pamphlet prepared by the Staff College, Camberley, p. 3. No other source has any clear discussion of the requirements levied on the division.
3. For a unit history see B. H. Liddell Hart, *The Tanks, Volume II*.
4. The unit history is in R.J.B. Sellar, *The Fife and Forfar Yeomanry 1919–1965*.
5. R.H.W.S. Hastings, *The Rifle Brigade in the Second World War 1939–1945* (Aldershot: Gale and Polden, 1950) I have based my narrative of the 8 RB on Colonel D. M. Stileman who was the commander of 11 platoon, G company, 8 RB at Goodwood and a participant in the battlefield tour.
6. *BAOR Battlefield Tour*, p. 13.

the 29th Armoured Brigade but to the west, i.e., on the Caen side. The infantry battalions of the brigade would be responsible for clearing and holding the villages of Cuverville and Demouville, which would have been largely destroyed by the aerial bombardment, until backup units from the Canadian Corps could advance and take over.[7] To support the infantry in this attack, the divisional armoured reconnaissance regiment, the 2nd Northamptonshire Yeomanry, which had been trained only in the reconnaissance role and not to cooperate with ground troops, was hurriedly retrained to work with infantry and assigned to this mop-up operation.[8]

Each of the armoured divisions in Goodwood had an armoured car regiment attached to it, and these were to be used to exploit and patrol the areas exposed by the attack of the divisions. The regiment attached to the 11th was the Inns of Court Regiment, which was to employ two of its four squadrons to patrol considerably in advance of the remainder of the British forces, along a line from St. Andre sur Orne through Bretteville sur Laize and St. Sylvain east to Vimont (British left flank). This was completely on the other side of Bourguebus Ridge and in the midst of the German artillery, although the planners, of course, could not know that.[9]

---

7. The only regimental history from this brigade that I have been able to locate is P. K. Kemp, *The History of the 4th Battalion, the King's Own Shropshire Light Infantry (T.A.) 1745–1945*. This battalion was in reserve in the initial attack.
8. General G. P. B. Roberts, 7 June 1971: conversation.
9. Targets of this type were normal for an armoured car regiment, which would use its speed and silence to penetrate enemy lines and reconnoiter rear areas.

After the capture of le Mesnil Frementel, the 11th Armoured would move on to its second-phase objectives. The 29th Armoured Brigade would move straight up the ridge to its final objective on the line of Bras-Verrieres-Rocquancourt, just over the crest beyond the Caen-Falaise road. This objective was well past the first villages on the ridge, Hubert Folie and Bourguebus. The 29th would also be required to hold the area around Cramesnil on its left flank until the 7th Armoured Division had advanced between the 11th and the Guards to carry on the attack. In this phase the 159th Infantry Brigade remained at Demouville until the Canadians on their right flank, along the Orne in the Caen suburbs, had captured Giberville, thus securing the western (right) flank. After this had happened, the infantry of the 11th Armoured Division could move forward to the Verrieres-Rocquancourt area,[10] to form a firm base with the tanks that had preceded it.

The Guards Armoured Division, which was to be the second division through the gap, had a role similar to that of the 11th—securing an area on Bourguebus Ridge with definite objectives and no major exploitation. In the first phase of the Guards operation, the division would relieve the elements of 29th Armoured Brigade that would be screening Cagny; and the 5th Guards Armoured Brigade, the armoured portion of the division, would then attack the village. The armoured reconnaissance regiment of

---

10. According to General G. P. B. Roberts, this movement of the infantry brigade was not specified in his orders, and in fact the corps commander held up the advance of the brigade that afternoon.

the Guards Division, the 2nd (Armoured) Battalion, The Welsh Guards,[11] would perform a classic reconnaissance task by masking Emieville on the left flank while the brigade dealt with Cagny.

After Cagny was neutralized, and with the 29th Armoured Brigade continuing its attack onto the ridge, one battalion[12] of tanks (of the Guards Armoured) would advance to Vimont, with its flanks covered by a squadron of tanks of the Welsh Guards operating on the right flank between Cagny and Chicheboville which in turn would be very close to the left flank of 11th Armoured near Cramesnil.

In the third phase the 32nd Guards Brigade, the infantry brigade of the Guards Armoured Division, would move from the salient area to Cagny, relieving the armour which could then move on to Vimont. The infantry would secure and clear Cagny, while the armour would reinforce the battalion that had taken the area. When Cagny was cleared, the 32nd Guards Brigade would proceed to Vimont and form a firm base, as would the 159th on the western flank of the newly created salient. When this occurred, the tanks of the 5th Guards Armoured Brigade would withdraw to an area astride the Caen-Vimont road to refuel and resupply while awaiting any further orders.

---

11. L. F. Ellis, *The Welsh Guards at War*. Major Ellis also wrote the official history.
12. In the Guards Armoured Division, the titles were more than usually confusing. Although they were armoured, the tank units retained the infantry term battalion but adopted the mounted terms squadron and troop, so that there was B Company, 1st Battalion, The Welsh Guards and a B Squadron, 2nd Battalion, The Welsh Guards. To further complicate the situation, there was no A Company, 1st Battalion. The company was called Prince of Wales Company.

The orders issued to these two divisions were similar and contained identical weaknesses. While both had limited and well-defined objectives, the divisions had to be employed piecemeal which was to be a fatal flaw in the plan. In each case, while the armoured brigade was capturing one village, the infantry was a village behind, securing the last objective. This prevented the armoured units from dealing with much of the resistance, although more accompanying infantry would not have helped a great deal in the tank-versus-tank fight which finally stopped the 11th on Bourguebus Ridge. It is also interesting to note that when the objective had finally been achieved, it was the infantry brigade that was called forward to form a base to resist counterattacks and behind which the tanks prepared for any further attacks.

The 7th Armoured Division, the most experienced and equipped with the fastest tanks, was to remain in the rear throughout the early stages of the battle. When the routes across the river and through the airborne salient were free,[13] the 22nd Armoured Brigade would deploy in the le Mesnil Frementel area and then advance on an axis running from Four to La Hogue. The objectives were Secqueville, La Campagne and Cramesnil. When these areas were taken, the division's infantry brigade, the 131st, would advance and form the usual firm base at Secqueville.

Thus at the end of the moves given in the initial orders for Operation Goodwood, the three armoured divisions would be atop Bourguebus Ridge in a rough

---

13. General Roberts, 7 June 1971: Conversation. *BAOR Battlefield Tour*, Ellis, and Wilmot are all unclear on the timing of this move.

semicircle, with the most-worn armoured division, the 11th, on the longest but relatively secure front, and the freshest and fastest division positioned alongside the road to Falaise, pointed directly at that important road junction. Even if the tanks were unable to proceed further, their mere presence near this crucial road junction would have the desired effect on German dispositions by drawing the German armoured reserves to this front to protect against the threat of these divisions.

The only major objection voiced to these orders was by General Roberts of the 11th. He opposed not having his infantry brigade with him in the attack, and he wanted other forces to take Cuverville and Demouville while all of 11th Armoured Division attacked the major objectives on Bourguebus Ridge.[14] This request was denied by the corps, and the divisions prepared to execute the orders as received.

When the concentration of forces for Goodwood began, the three divisions were widely separated. The 11th Armoured Division was half way between Caen and Bayeux, closest to the salient; 7th Armoured Division was north of Tilly-sur-Seulles close behind the Epsom salient, where it had most recently been in action; and the freshly arrived Guards were two miles east of Bayeux.[15] These units, with 3,500 vehicles each, had to be moved to the eastern end of the salient with maximum security and in time for the beginning of the operation: this obviously would be a

---
14. General Roberts, 7 June 1971: talk at Staff College Battlefield Tour.
15. *BAOR Battlefield Tour*, p. 15.

rather difficult task. In addition to the length of the move and the need for security, all three divisions had to cross the supply routes of the two corps already in the area, who would also be attacking as part of Goodwood; also, once the divisions arrived at the Canal de Caen and the River Orne, there were only three bridges on which to cross these water barriers.[16] To deal with all these problems and to make all the necessary arrangements, VIII Corps set up a Corps Traffic office directly under the Brigadier General Staff.[17] The plan was basically one of careful control and coordination to move men and equipment to the proper place at the proper time. On the western side of the waterways, six tracks were laid out for the divisions—one "tracked" vehicle route and one "wheeled" vehicle route leading to each of the three bridges. On the Bourguebus side, the luxury of separate tracks was dispensed with and everybody moved up to the gap on common routes.[18] There was an elaborate system under the corps assistant provost marshal to control movements by radio and to have an answer to every question.

With such planning, VIII Corps was able to move successfully all the needed forces to their required positions. The 11th Armoured Division was moved entirely into the salient, and the other two divisions were lined up along the tracks just before the bridges

---

16. G. S. Jackson, *Operations Eighth Corps*, p. 90. See also *Bridging: Normandy to Berlin* for photographs and details of the bridges.
17. Jackson, p. 90. The British have a different staff system than the United States. The Brigadier General Staff (B.G.S.) is roughly the chief of staff of a corps or higher.
18. Jackson, p. 91; *BAOR Battlefield Tour*, p. 15.

into the salient. Prepared for their missions, they were positioned with their armoured brigades in front and in the order for their attack, Guards and then 7th. The Guards would advance at H hour as soon as the 11th began to clear the salient, and the 7th would move out an hour later to allow two Canadian brigades to pass forward to their own attack.[19]

The 11th Armoured Division began its move on the night of 16 July, and the divisional headquarters and the infantry brigade were in the salient around Amfreville that night.[20] The 29th Armoured Brigade moved to the west bank on the sixteenth but waited until the following night to move into the salient,[21] arriving at its concentration area at 0100 on the eighteenth.

Having arrived at its starting positions, 11th Armoured Division had six hours and forty-five minutes to make final preparations for the attacks. The two night marches had been extremely wearing on the troops, since the warm days and enemy activity had, to a large extent, prevented the troops from sleeping during the day. On their arrival in the salient, the men had to prepare the vehicles for the next morning's attack. Around 0230 the commanders conducted a reconnaissance of the minefield gap and,

---

19. Jackson, p. 91.
20. *Taurus Pursuant, A History of 11th Armoured Division*, p. 23.
21. L. F. Ellis, *Victory in the West:Volume I. The Battle of Normandy*, p. 338; *Taurus Pursuant*, p. 23; and Major W. H. Close, MC and Bar, Late Royal Tank Regiment and Royal Electrical and Mechanical Engineers, talk at 1971 Staff College Tour. Major Close commanded A Squadron 3rd RTR, one of the lead squadrons of 11th Armoured Division. Jackson, p. 91, incorrectly states that all of 11th was in the salient by the night of the 16th/17th.

when they returned, the armoured regiments moved up to the start line with the tanks nose to tail. All was ready.[22]

At 0530 the supporting bombardment began and continued until H hour. To the troops in their tanks, it seemed as though the enemy must surely be destroyed by the weight of the barrage.[23] There were also friendly casualties, however, as a short round killed one of the lead squadron commanders in the Third Royal Tanks.[24] At H hour, 0745, the great advance began, lead by A and B Squadron of the Third Royal Tank Regiment—thirty-eight tanks against Bourguebus Ridge and the defending German army. The tanks advanced in box formations, each four-tank "troop" in a square with the 75mm-gun Shermans in front and the more heavily armed Fireflys to the rear.[25] They were also accompanied by special-purpose tanks: a squadron of minesweeping "Flails" of the 22nd Dragoons and a half squadron of Armoured Vehicles, Royal Engineers (AVREs) tanks with powerful demolition guns which would be used to blow holes in the railway embankment.[26] When the tanks got beyond the minefield, the formations opened to an 800-yard front, and by 1030 they had passed le Mesnil Frementel where they captured 134 prisoners.

---

22. Major Close: 1971 battlefield tour.
23. Major Close; *Taurus Pursuant*, p. 23.
24. Major Close.
25. Major Close. This was to protect them against being immediately knocked out.
26. Major Close. The so-called "Funnies" belonged to 79th Armoured Division, an administrative headquarters.

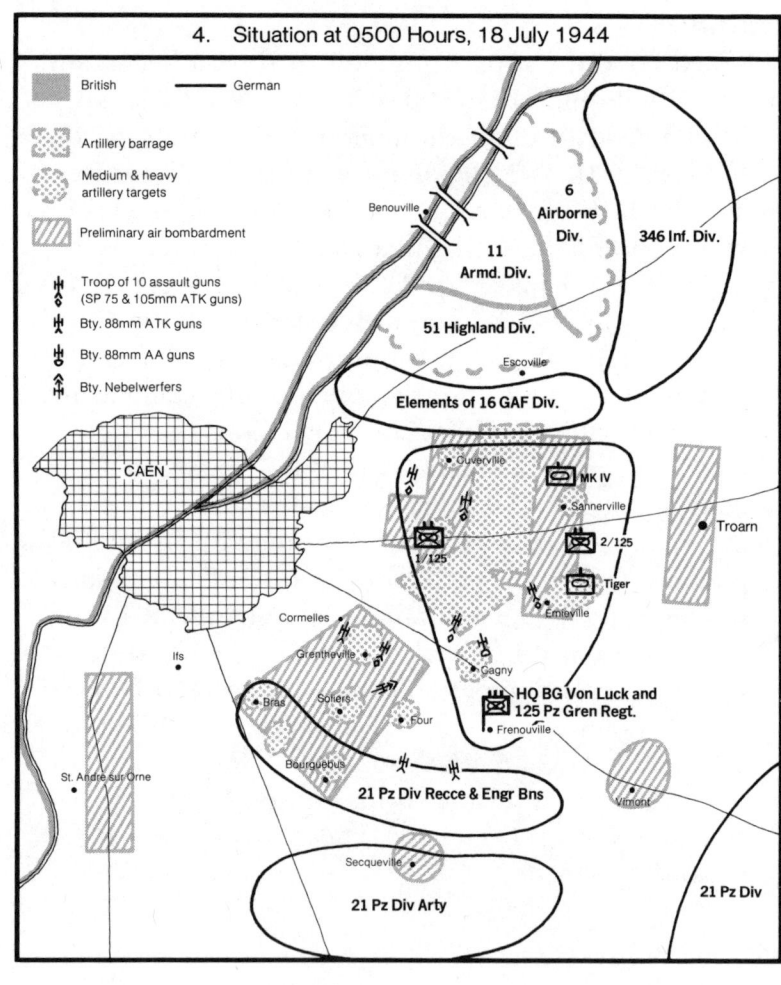

Already, however, things had begun to go awry. The first two armoured regiments had gotten through the minefield and deployed, but the reserve regiment, the 23rd Hussars, fell well behind and instead of being 300 yards to the rear were a mile behind the lead regiments and thus unable to assist them properly.[27] But the real problems occurred in the 159th Brigade. This had not been a particularly efficient unit in the past, and General Roberts had relieved the brigade commander shortly before Goodwood. There were also two new battalion commanders. In addition, as previously mentioned, the armoured support for the brigade's attack on Cuverville and Demouville was the 2nd Northamptonshire Yeomanry, which was not trained for infantry cooperation. Consequently, on the morning of the eighteenth, the job of clearing the two villages took much longer than expected. This was due in part to the quick recovery of the German defenders from the bombardment, but even more so to the slowness of the Canadians who were to relieve the 159th. General Roberts had accompanied the armoured brigade since he felt that this force had the more difficult task,[28] but apparently the commander of the infantry brigade was not as forceful as he might have been. Events occurred such as the commander of the 4th

---

27. Peter Walter: talk at 1971 Staff College Battlefield Tour. Mr. Walter was a captain and second in command of C Squadron 23rd Hussars in Goodwood.
28. General Roberts, 7 June 1971: talk.

Kings' Shropshire Light Infantry taking an hour and a half to find the brigadier.[29]

The first major opposition to the advance occurred as the 29th Armoured Brigade passed Cagny, where there were a number of 88mm guns. The 3rd Tanks escaped damage as did the lead elements of the Fife and Forfar Yeomanry, but C Squadron was destroyed by these guns which arrived after the British began to pass. The cause of the tank casualties is still a matter of great controversy. Most published sources claim that German Tiger tanks did the damage, but there is conclusive evidence against this assertion.

The first German troops encountered in the attack were those of the 16th Luftwaffe Field Division, who surrendered with little resistance after the debilitating effects of the bombing. Behind them lay elements of the 125th Panzergrenadier Regiment of the 21st Panzer Division formed into Kampfgruppe Luck. Luck was just returning from a three-day pass to Paris and was not in the area under bombardment.[30] He quickly rallied the troops and placed his headquarters in the gap between Emieville and

---

29. General Roberts; Kemp, *History of 4KSLI*, p. 89. Kemp, while admitting the failure on the part of the KSLI CO, says the commander of 29th Armoured Brigade took three hours to find Roberts at the height of the battle.
30. Oberst a.D. Hans von Luck, talk at 1971 Battlefield Tour. Luck's full story was that he had had a great time in Paris and "Honi soit qui mal y pense." He came over the ridge just in time to see the bombers attack and did not even have time to change his uniform before singlehandedly stopping the British. He most certainly played a major role in the battle, but he undoubtedly enjoys claiming an even larger role.

Cagny, reinforcing that locale although there was in fact no threat to that area from the 11th Armoured Division. Slightly to the rear of Cagny, Luck then discovered a Luftwaffe anti-aircraft battery that was not taking part in the battle, and he persuaded the commander to move into the woods on the northern edge of the village.[31] These German guns apparently were the ones that did all the damage to the 29th Armoured Brigade. The only Tiger tank unit in this area was the 503rd SS Heavy Tank Battalion consisting of one company of Tiger II tanks and two of Tiger Is. They had been heavily hit by the bombing although few tanks were totally destroyed. In the 3rd Company, bombs destroyed four tanks, including one which was turned over by the blast effect, but the majority were disabled by the sheer weight of the bombing.[32] Tanks that were untouched by fragments had their engine intakes clogged with dirt, gun barrels full of debris, and the optics on their guns completely knocked out of alinement. In the company, fifteen men were killed, two committed suicide and one became insane from the effects of the bombs. By hard work, the troops restored thirteen tanks to operation and used them against the British, but by the

---

31. Luck claims he forced the reluctant Luftwaffe officer to move his guns at the point of a Luger. He also says he told the artilleryman he would shoot him right there or else the man could take his chances with the British and Luck would recommend him for a medal.
32. Hauptmann von Rosen, commander of 3rd Company, 503 SS Heavy Tank Battalion at Goodwood: recorded talk presented at battlefield tour, June 1971.

time these were repaired, the 11th must have been past Cagny.[33] All but one of these Tiger tanks were destroyed in ground combat before nightfall.

Despite the devastating effects of the 88s, General Roberts, thinking Cagny was strongly held, followed his orders and screened the village while continuing the attack.[34] By 1010, 3rd RTR was in the vicinity of Grentheville. At 1115, a troop of the 2nd Fife and Forfar was abreast of Bourguebus village.[35] Reached six hours after the start of the battle, this point was to be the farthest south that anyone penetrated in Goodwood. Despite the progress of the tanks, the infantry was still clearing villageu to the rear. The armour was held up in some cases by the need for infantry to come forward and take over before the first group could advance. The bridgehead was now so congested that movement was difficult, and German artillery was beginning to put counterbattery fire in the area.

In the meantime the advance of the 11th Armoured Division along the ridge was halting in the early afternoon, as all three armoured regiments moved up to the area of Soliers and Four. Here they

---

33. Von Rosen; von Luck; Ellis, *Victory in the West*, p. 340; and Liddell Hart, *The Tanks*, p. 364. Also, many of the unit histories support the Tiger-tanks theory.
34. Luck commented to General Roberts during a talk at the battlefield tour that this was his big mistake and that he (Luck) would never have bypassed Cagny. General Roberts admits that perhaps he shouldn't have done this. Luck claims there were four guns and eight infantry men in Cagny at this early stage.
35. Jackson, *Operations Eighth Corps*, p. 95.

The Battle: First Day / 85

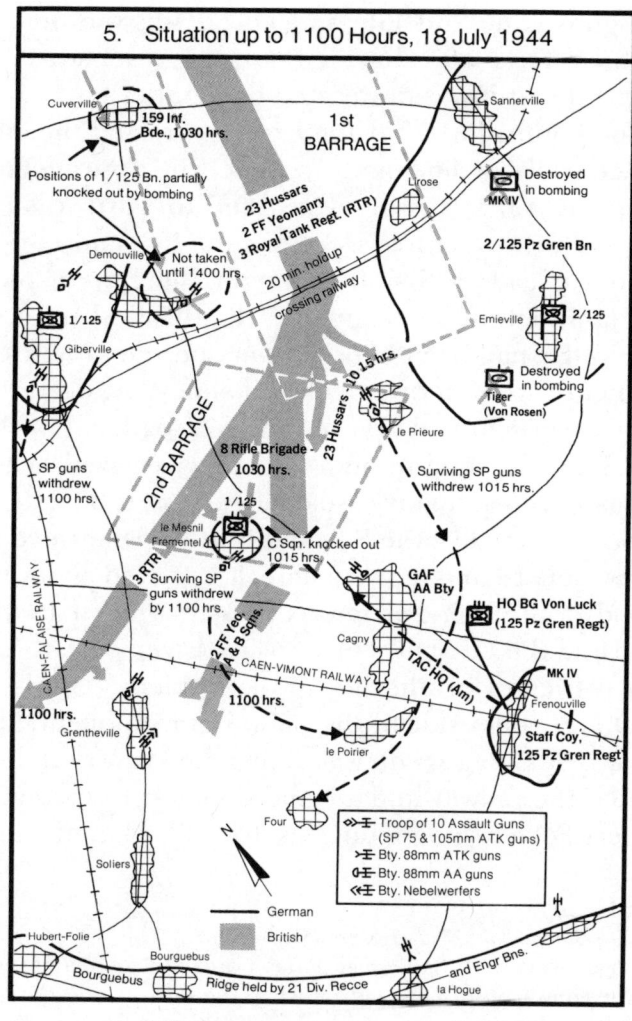

5. Situation up to 1100 Hours, 18 July 1944

met heavy resistance from German tanks and anti-tank guns. The 2nd Fife and Forfar was the first to feel the effects; after having lost nearly a squadron at Cagny, the unit was devastated by Panther tanks and anti-tank guns just after their troops crossed the embanked railway line and headed for Bourguebus. When the 23rd Hussars was called forward to support, the men were told by one of the Fife and Forfar squadron leaders that he thought there were only four tanks left in his regiment.[36] By this time most of the Fireflys had been knocked out and the armoured regiments were more or less helpless against the heavier German tanks. When the full regiment of the 23rd Hussars came up in a line, they received heavy German fire and many casualties ensued. C Squadron of the Hussars, like the Fife and Forfar, penetrated as far as Soliers and Four where it received a severe "bloody ‚ose," losing all but six tanks.[37] Then both this force and the Fife and Forfar were driven back to the area between Grentheville and le Poirier.

On the other side of the railway embankment, 3rd Royal Tank Regiment was doing no better. It had crossed the railway and advanced almost to Bras and Hubert Folie by noon, but was driven back to the line

---

36. *The Story of the 23rd Hussars 1940–1946.* p. 75.
37. Peter Walter at Battlefield Tour. Captain Walter took over the command of C Squadron when the squadron leader was killed. He won a Distinguished Service Order for his rallying of the tanks and the stubborn fight he conducted, including the destruction of a counterattack with artillery fire, which he called in by saying "Hello this is Peter Walter, I need some artillery fire," on the BBC frequency. The BBC relayed the message.

of the embankment by 1400. There is no cover between the embankment and the villages, and so the regiment either had to take enormous losses in trying to capture Hubert Folie without adequate support, or had to fall back to the railway. A patrol from the 8th Rifle Brigade did in fact go down the main street of Hubert Folie to see if the Germans still held the village, only to discover that the Germans were very much in possession.

By this time the 11th Armoured Division had completely penetrated the 21st Panzer and was fighting the 1st SS Panzer Division which had come up over the ridge. The 1st SS Panzer was fresher than the 21st and was also much better equipped. While the 21st had a great deal of French equipment, the SS had modern German vehicles, especially Panther tanks.

Thus ended the great charge of the armoured divisions. Much of the rest of Goodwood was simply clearing up the line, making small advances or resisting counterattacks. No more great gains would be made in this operation. The massive support and the lavish use of all types of ordnance had foundered in the quick reactions of the Germans and the slow movement of the three ponderous British armoured divisions.

After the afternoon of the eighteenth, the role of the 11th Armoured Division declined, and the story of the failure of Operation Goodwood to achieve its territorial objectives centers on the other two armoured divisions.

CHAPTER VI

Conclusion of the Battle

BY THE AFTERNOON of the eighteenth, the operation was definitely beginning to bog down: the 11th Armoured Division and the Guards were running into heavy resistance on the ridge, and the 7th Armoured Division was not making much progress against the congestion of the rear areas in its attempt to gain the front line. General O'Connor was urging on the troops, but no one was to make spectacular gains as the 11th had done that morning. The hour of the great attack was over, and the quick reactions of the Germans and the growing congestion of the salient complicated every British action.

By the night of the eighteenth, the situation required a large-scale reorganization. While the various commanders attempted to work out this problem, many units were still trying to move forward in the congestion of the salient. Matters were not helped by spasmodic German air raids which caused some casualties. After extensive reorganization, an attack was made on the nineteenth. This attack made substantial gains and several villages fell to the British armour. The attacks of the peripheral corps on the nineteenth were also reasonably successful.

On the twentieth the VIII Corps was given one last task, the capture of Bourguebus village, and that afternoon the units began to hand over their positions to the infantry corps on either flank and withdraw. The opportunity of a great armoured breakthrough was over and, as if to reinforce the point, a torrential rain began to fall that afternoon which would have ended armoured operations in any case. Over the next three days, the infantry made minor adjustments and the armoured divisions withdrew to refit and make up their battle losses.

Throughout the battle the Germans reacted quickly and efficiently on the small unit level and more slowly but still effectively in the higher echelons. The immediate reaction was a quick marshaling of the available resources and the successful use of these units to hold the British to their initial gains. By the twentieth, however, it was obvious that the Germans were no more capable than the British of mounting any major attack in this area and that both sides would have to be content with the gains made by the British.

The beginning of this second phase was on the

afternoon of the eighteenth. The 29th Armoured Brigade held a line overlooking Bras, Hubert Folie and Soliers.[1] Just at dusk a final attack was made on the Fife and Forfars by six Tigers,[2] and after that the regiment was withdrawn and replaced by the 23rd Hussars, who went into a protective formation for the night.[3] The 159th Infantry Brigade was considerably to the rear near le Mesnil Frementel, where the 4th King's Shropshire Light Infantry spent the night.[4] The 8th Rifle Brigade was in Grentheville. In this position it was occupying the same area as the armoured brigade of the 7th Armoured Division. In the words of the historian of the 11th Armoured Division: "The infantry had had a hard but successful day; it was the armoured brigade that had borne the brunt of the fighting."[5] The 11th Armoured Division had lost 126 tanks and 336 men in return for seven miles of captured enemy terrain.[6]

The Guards Armoured Division moved from its starting position somewhat behind schedule but soon caught up and was waiting behind the tail of the 29th Armoured Brigade by 0945, when the 29th was still

---

1. *Taurus Pursuant, A History of 11th Armoured Division*, p. 25.
2. *Taurus Pursuant*, p. 26; R.J.B. Sellar, *The Fife and Forfar Yeomanry 1919–1956*, p. 170.
3. *The Story of the 23rd Hussars 1940–1946*, p. 78.
4. P.K. Kemp, *The History of the 4th Battalion, The King's Own Shropshire Light Infantry (T.A.) 1745–1945*, p. 90.
5. *Taurus Pursuant*, p. 25-26.
6. *British Army of the Rhine—Battlefield Tour* p. 39. for tanks; and Jackson, p. 103, for personnel. Wilmot, p. 360 gives this figure also, without source. However, his papers contain a copy of the BAOR tour book.

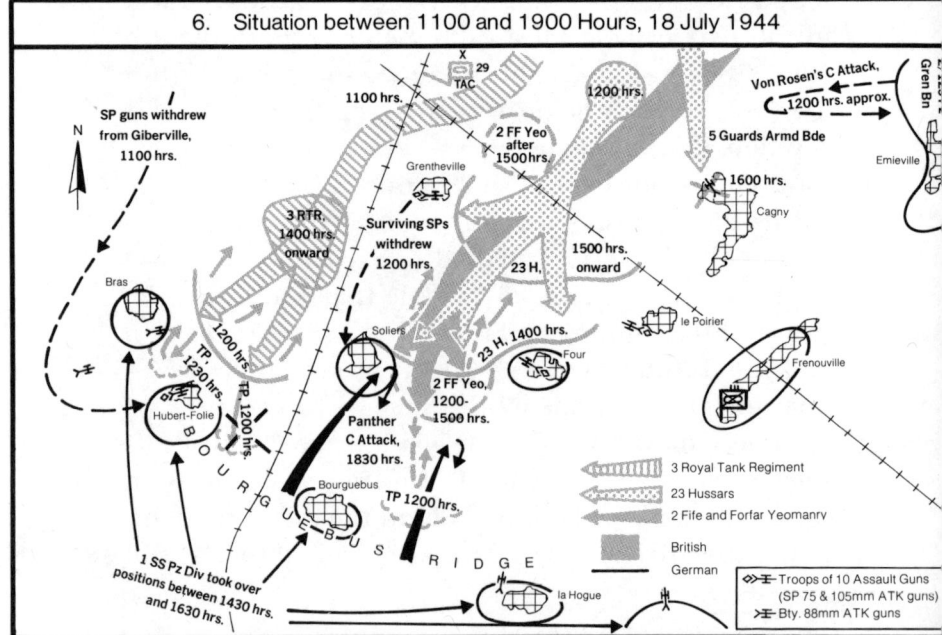

6. Situation between 1100 and 1900 Hours, 18 July 1944

involved near Cagny.[7] Each of the armoured battalions of the 5th Guards Armoured Brigade had a company from the motor battalion, 1st Battalion the Grenadier Guards,[8] attached to provide instant infantry support. Feeling that nothing could have survived the bombing, the troops were eager to move.[9]

The 5th Guards Armoured Brigade made its first contact with the Germans at Cagny. The 2nd Battalion the Grenadier Guards ran into the first resistance which they believed came from Tiger tanks. The fire may well have been from the vehicles of the 503rd SS Heavy Tank Battalion, which were operational again, or possibly from the 88s that Oberst Luck placed in Cagny. In any case this unexpected development caused a severe delay as it took the rest of the afternoon for elements of the division to capture Cagny. Meanwhile, the failure of the tail of the Guards Armoured Division to move was causing great congestion, and O'Connor ordered the division to move up toward Vimont as fast as possible. As a result the armoured regiments had to sidestep around Cagny which further increased the congestion.[10] In addition,

---

7. G. S. Jackson, *Operations Eighth Corps*, p. 96. Also Captain the Earl of Rosse and Colonel E. R Hill, *The Story of the Guards Armoured Division*, p. 38, and G. L. Verney, *The Guards Armoured Division*, p. 40.
8. Jackson, p. 96. See also Nigel Nicholson and Patrick Forbes, *The Grenadier Guards in the War of 1939–1945, Vol. 1*, for a regimental history.
9. Major General A.H.S. Adair, commander of Guards Armoured Division at Goodwood, June 1971: recorded talk at Staff College Battlefield Tour.
10. General Adair; Rosse, p. 38-39.

this delay was hurting the 11th Division which was having to secure both flanks and thus was unable to concentrate its forces for a single thrust at any objective. Because of the backup at Cagny, only one regiment of the Guards was able to reach the flank of the 11th that afternoon. This was the 1st Armoured Battalion, the Coldstream Guards.[11]

From this point, the story of the Guards Armoured Division on the first day is similar to that of the 11th Armoured Division. Both at Cagny and near le Poirier where the Coldstream Guards were fighting, the battle became one of trying to overcome or outmaneuver the Germans who were in superior positions, had superior guns, and were supported by more heavily armoured tanks than the British. It was not until 1800 that the Grenadiers finally took Cagny. The rest of the division was able to move up and support the Coldstream Guards who then took le Poirier, although the defenses of Frenouville were so strong that the village resisted all attempts to capture it that day.

One of the major problems of the Guards Armoured Division was that the 32nd Guards Infantry Brigade spent the first day "in a deadly, dusty, crawling procession of transport, bumping along through gaps in minefields feeling indecently exposed to bursting shells and wondering why those in front did not get more of a move on."[12] It was not until evening

---

11. Rosse, p. 41; Verney, *Guards Armoured Division*, p. 41. See also Michael Howard and John Sparrow, *The Coldstream Guards 1920–1946*.
12. D. H. Erskine, *The Scots Guards*, p. 339.

that the 32nd Brigade caught up with the armour. These troops, with the 1st Battalion the Welsh Guards, were then able to take Cagny. Having captured the village, they occupied it that night, although as a result of the bombing "truly Cagny was no longer a place for human habitation."[13] The 2nd Welsh Guards remained in the Emieville area while the rest of the division spent the night south of Cagny. They were no closer to taking Frenouville than the armoured elements had been that day. The Guards had not accomplished much in their first day of battle, most of which had been spent in what one historian called "this unsatisfactory exchange of shots."[14] On the eighteenth the Guards lost sixty tanks and 137 men for the capture of Cagny.[15]

The story of the 7th Armoured Division on 18 July is largely one of congestion in the salient and delays caused by the slow advance of the 11th Armoured Division. There is some question as to how energetically General Erskine pushed the advance. Chester Wilmot is the main proponent of this view and says:

> Erskine regarded the whole operation as a gross abuse of armour and seemed determined to keep his tanks out of the maelstrom as long as possible. In response to pleas from

---

13. L. F. Ellis, *The Welsh Guards at War*, p. 176.
14. Major D.J.L. FitzGerald, *History of the Irish Guards in the Second World War*, p. 378.
15. General Adair; both divisional histories (for the tanks). Jackson, p. 96 (for the men).

Roberts and exhortations from O'Connor, Erskine maintained that there was no room to get through between the 11th and the Guards.[16]

Whatever the command situation was, the battlefield was enormously congested and only the 5th Royal Tank Regiment, which was the lead regiment of 22nd Armoured Brigade, went into action on the first day of Goodwood. This force fought a sharp action near Grentheville after which it took up a defensive position there. The other tanks of the division were roughly in line: the 1st RTR just east of the 5th; and the third regiment, the 4th County of London Yeomanry, further east. The 159th Infantry Brigade from the 11th occupied the villages in this area. In this day of battle the 7th Armoured Division had lost twelve men and six tanks, all from the 5th Royal Tanks.[17]

On the left flank of the armoured attack, I Corps had launched an attack against the main town on

---

16. Chester Wilmot, *The Struggle for Europe*, p. 359. Many historians disparage Wilmot as a reliable source. I have been told by a former member of the official history team that he worked alongside them, and I have examined his papers which were left to Sir Basil Liddell Hart and which contain several not generally available sources. I feel that Wilmot had access to virtually everything the official team did, without the restriction of being a civil servant.
17. G. L. Verney, *The Desert Rats*, p. 205. See also *History of the 7th Armoured Division, June 1943–July 1945*. Jackson, p. 103, gives forty-eight casualties from all causes, probably including accidents and artillery in the rear areas.

that flank, Troarn. The operations order stated: "Attack and hold the area of Touffreville, Sannerville, Banneville la Campagne, Manneville, Cuillerville, le Quai, and Troarn."[18] These villages formed a triangle in the area due east of Cuverville and Demouville and were a prime target of the preliminary aerial bombardment; Sannerville, for example, virtually was obliterated by bombs and preplanned artillery barrages. Since this was to be largely an infantry operation, the requirements for preserving the terrain that applied to the main battlefront did not apply here.

The three brigades of the 3rd Division each had a separate task: the 8th Brigade, clearing Touffreville and Sannerville; the 185th, passing farther south to attack le Quai and Cuillerville; and the 9th Brigade, attacking east to Troarn. The 3rd British Division thus made a three-pronged attack, with the easternmost prong parallel to the main thrust of VIII Corps and about 1,500 yards east of it, and the westernmost virtually at right angles to the armoured thrust. The 8th Brigade was the first in action since its objectives in the center were closest to the start line in the southwest corner of the airborne salient. Touffreville had not been completely hit by the bombs destined for it and thus held out until around six in the evening, but Sannerville and Banneville la Campagne were quickly captured for "those Germans left conscious were far too dazed to offer any resistance."[19] The 185th Brigade had the longest distance

---

18. Norman Scarfe, *Assault Division*, p. 116.
19. *Ibid*., p. 118.

to travel and even though the troops were mounted on the backs of tanks, an expedient not used in the main attack, they had not reached the objectives by night because of heavy resistance. At last light the brigade was still fighting in the vicinity of Manneville west of its objectives. The 9th Brigade pushed steadily toward Troarn and consolidated for the night a mile west of the town itself. On this flank, just north of the 3rd Division, 51st Highland Division also made a small attack with 152nd Brigade. This force took its objectives, several small woods on the flank of the 3rd Division, but suffered heavily from shell fire, which had caused most of the casualties on this flank. Some 500 casualties and eighteen tanks had been lost in this fight against elements of the 16th Luftwaffe Field Division and the 346th German Infantry Division.[20]

On the opposite flank, the Canadians were experiencing many of the problems encountered in the main thrust. The Canadian attack, Operation Atlantic, was launched simultaneously with Goodwood.[21] The Canadians would be concerned with capturing the area between the right flank of VIII Corps and the Orne River. The boundary with VIII Corps was a line roughly through St. Honorine la Chardonerette, Giberville, and Bras. In addition, the Canadians were to be prepared to capture this area, to bridge the Orne in Caen and to attack across the river straight

---

20. L. F. Ellis, *Victory in the West: Volume I. The Battle of Normandy*, p. 343.
21. C. P. Stacey, *The Victory Campaign*, pp. 170-71. This Canadian official history is the best available source on the Canadians. Most unit histories gloss over Goodwood in favor of the Battle of the Falaise Gap.

up the end of Bourguebus Ridge, also taking Ifs and Verrieres if the opportunity presented itself. The 3rd Canadian Infantry Division would make the initial attack with one brigade as a reserve and the other two, the 8th and 9th Canadian Infantry Brigades, as the main attack force. The 8th Brigade crossed into the salient on the seventeenth, but the 9th was the unit which had to pass over the Orne bridges between the Guards and the 7th Armoured Division the next morning.

The target area, the suburbs of Caen at Colombelles and Faubourg de Vaucelles, was heavily built up, and Colombelles was an industrial center with a large steelworks. They were heavily damaged before the battle and received further attention that morning from both the bombers and four regiments of artillery. When the two lead battalions of the 8th Brigade attacked, they found that this damage only increased the difficulty of their task for the Germans defended the ruins of the steelworks with great tenacity. With the initial check at Colombelles, one battalion, the Queen's Own Rifles of Canada, shifted to the left and moved against Giberville, where the resistance was lighter; the town was taken by late afternoon. While elements of the 8th Brigade continued to fight in the industrial area, not clearing the steelworks until the next morning, the second brigade, the 9th, bypassed this fighting and attacked Vaucelles. By night, this force had only succeeded in taking part of the town.

As the initial problems were occurring in Colombelles, General Simonds, commander of II Canadian Corps, ordered the third brigade of the division, 7th Canadian Infantry Brigade, to attack across the river from Caen into Vaucelles, if the resistance was light. Since the bulk of the Germans were probably busy with the attack from the north, the crossing was relatively easy. By nightfall, the Regina Rifle Regiment also was established in Vaucelles.

The operations of the 2nd Canadian Infantry Division were further west: one brigade attacking Louvigny, which was west of the Orne, after the Orne turns due south at the western end of Caen; and the other brigade attacking the far western end of Vaucelles. The 4th Canadian Infantry Brigade began its mission in early evening and by dark was just north of Louvigny. The 5th Brigade of the division waited until the Germans were hopefully distracted by the action at Louvigny and then sent the Black Watch of Canada to attack Vaucelles from the rear. This operation, starting at 2215, went well and by morning of the nineteenth this force linked up with the Regina Rifle Regiment.[22] The Germans now had to face the enemy on three sides in Vaucelles. A main benefit of the success of these operations was that the Canadians were able to bridge the Orne within the confines of the city of Caen and no longer needed to worry about the limited access to the salient.

Throughout the day, the Germans reacted effectively to the attack. We have already seen how 125th Panzergrenadier Regiment quickly responded with a tough defense. The 272nd Infantry Division, facing the Canadians, while awed by the bombing did not seem to be greatly dismayed by the subsequent attack.

---

22. *Ibid.*, p. 172.

THE BATTLE

The beginning of Operation Goodwood. Cromwell tanks of the 2nd Battalion, Welsh Guards, move forward at dawn on July 18. The long, night approach march required by the small size of the airborne salient was a major problem in Goodwood planning.

Goodwood terrain. Tanks and armoured troop carriers of the 11th Armoured Division in the rolling terrain leading to Bourguebus Ridge. This area is typical of the Goodwood battlefield. Most open land was planted in wheat (called corn in British accounts), with tree lines and occasional groves dividing the plain.

Sherman tanks preparing to advance during Goodwood. The visibility of the tanks is apparent.

Tanks and tank crews of the 2nd Fife and Forfar Yeomanry with infantry of the 2nd Battalion, The Monmouthshire Regiment, riding on the tanks. These two regiments, elements of the 11th Armoured Division, fought separately in Goodwood: the Fife and Forfars led the left prong of the initial attack while the Monmouths followed up and secured Cuverville and Demouville. The first tank in the background is a standard Sherman and the second a Firefly with a 17-pounder gun. The four tanks parked along the edge of the field represent one troop of the four in each company.

A Company, 1st Battalion, The Welsh Guards, Guards Armoured Division, in action near Cagny. A Company was a lead company in the final assault which took Cagny. Burdened with the typical combat load of British infantry, the guardsmen have taken cover in a roadside ditch. The man pointing is an officer, Major J.D.A. Syrett, the company commander but scarcely distinguishable from his men. He was killed near Cagny on July 22 by shellfire.

Congestion was a major problem in Goodwood, as shown by the advance of elements of the Guards Armoured Division in Normandy. Visible on the road are lend-lease half-tracks which served as command vehicles, radio vehicles, fire direction centers and ambulances. On the other side of the road a signal jeep, with unit identification number 17, appears between two carriers. The infantry are members of the 1st Battalion, Welsh Guards.

The effects of the bombing. Banneville la Campagne, like other villages in the area, was heavily damaged in the preliminary bombing. Here an armoured bulldozer clears the Caen-Troarn road as it passes through the town.

A Sherman ARV I, standard British armoured recovery vehicle, tows a Sherman through the ruins of Bourguebus. The crucial question in many interpretations of Operation Goodwood is the number of tanks lost. Virtually all British tank losses were within the area captured and could be recovered and, if damage were not too severe, repaired. Thus many tanks, like this one, became casualties on the battlefield but were not losses.

The Germans fought hard and well, giving ground only as necessary.[23] Even the 16th Luftwaffe Field Division, which was the most heavily hit of the German units, managed to survive the bombing with both of its remaining regiments still functioning, although suffering heavy losses in personnel.[24] This unit was then destroyed in the fighting around Touffreville, Sannerville, and Troarn. But the major involvement was that of the armoured divisions under Panzergruppe West, the 21st and 1st SS Panzer Divisions, which reacted quickly to the attack. The Kriegstagbuch of Panzergruppe West exemplifies the calm professional way that all the Germans seem to have reacted. The divisions speedily rallied their subunits, analysed the situation and made requests for support and reinforcement. In particular, they devoted substantial efforts to maintaining communications and exchanging information.[25] This reaction was the key to the German success in limiting the gains of Goodwood.

The Germans struck one of their most devastating blows on the night of the eighteenth. Shortly before midnight, the Germans mounted an air raid on the salient, dropping most of their bombs on the rear echelon of the 11th Armoured Division and hitting

---

23. Martin Jenner, *Die 216/272 niedersachsische Infanterie-Division 1939–1945*, pp. 153-58.
24. *Foreign Military Studies*, Mss. B-284. "Die Zerschlangung der 16th Lw. Feld Div. an 18: 7.44" by Sievers, pp. 132-35.
25. The Kreigstagbuch is one of the *German Records Microfilmed at Alexandria, Virginia*, and is in Microfilm publication T-354, Roll 154, Frames 8713550-558.

many members of replacement tank crews, either survivors of the day's battle or fresh personnel.[26] They also hit the main headquarters of the division, further complicating the hurried reorganization that Roberts was trying to carry out. Other than this raid, the night was quiet and morning found the reorganized units ready for another attack.

For the 11th Armoured Division, 19 July was a slow day. General Roberts had informed corps and the other divisions that the 11th would not be ready to take offensive action before 1100. In fact, the 23rd Hussars and the 2nd Fife and Forfar Yeomanry spent the day in reserve, after their losses of the eighteenth. The 3rd Royal Tank Regiment was reorganized into three squadrons of ten tanks each, instead of the normal nineteen tanks in a squadron.[27] The other divisions made similar adjustments and waited for new orders. Corps orders for the nineteenth indicated modified objectives. General O'Connor wanted to consolidate and tidy up his front line before proceeding further. To accomplish this, 11th Armoured Division would attack and clear Bras and then Hubert Folie, starting at 1600. At 1700, the Guards Armoured Division would try again to take le Poirier and "exploit towards Frenouville but not attempt further operations toward Vimont."[28] At the same time the 7th Armoured Division, which was still very

---

26. Sellar, p. 171. The only definite figures are for the Fife and Forfars: six killed, forty-three wounded—twelve tank crews gone at one blow.
27. Major Close, June 1971: talk at the battlefield tour.
28. Jackson, p. 105. B. H. Liddell Hart, *The Tanks. Volume II*, p. 367, gives a rather different version involving an attack on the 3rd RTR as the cause of the late hour in this attack.

Conclusion of the Battle / 103

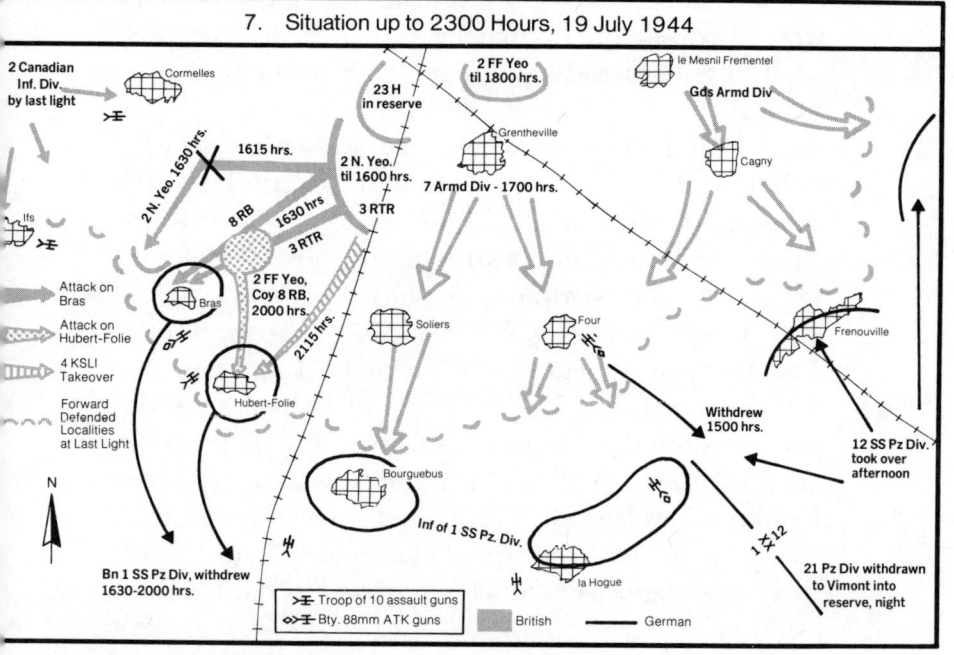

fresh, would finish clearing Soliers and then take Four and Bourguebus. If conditions were favorable after these villages were secured, then exploitation toward Verriers could be tried. While these attacks were going on, the infantry to the rear would clear the area already captured, making sure no pockets of resistance remained. O'Connor was thus becoming cautious after the losses of the previous day and wanted to be certain that he was in firm control of what he had already taken before continuing the offensive.

The attacks of the second day were all successful although the plans took some adjustment. The 11th Armoured Division attacked with the 3rd Royal Tanks and the 2nd Northamptonshire Yeomanry. Originally, the Northamptonshire Yeomanry was to take Bras; and the Royal Tanks, Hubert Folie. But the Yeomanry was held up in front of Bras, and the Tanks swung in on the flank and helped take the village where they captured a fresh battalion from the 1st SS Panzer Division which had just replaced a unit from the 21st Panzer. The Fife and Forfars were then called up to take Hubert Folie, which it did.[29] All three regiments were quickly replaced by battalions of infantry.

The Guards Armoured Division had few problems when the Welsh Guards took le Poirier, but the Coldstreams again were unable to take Frenouville. The 7th Armoured Division did not fare well either.

---

29. Sellar, p. 171, is very confused in assigning a previous attack to the Northamptonshire Yeomanry when there was not any previous attack. Moreover, the Yeomanry was at Bras.

Four and Soliers fell quickly to combined attacks, but Bourguebus continued to hold out although by dark it was surrounded. The 3rd British Infantry Division did even more poorly in the I Corps sector. After fighting all day, its troops were still unable to take Troarn, and losses were continually increasing not only from the attacks but from the incessant artillery and mortar fire.

The Canadians had minimal trouble in the operations carried out on their front. Cormelles and Fleury sur Orne were their new targets and these fell easily, as did the objectives that had not been taken on the previous day. The only trouble occurred at Ifs and was caused more by mortar fire than enemy resistance. On the twentieth, however, the Canadians were to have a much worse day as they conducted attacks on St. Andre sur Orne and Verrieres. St. Andre was captured, but the attack on Verrieres ran into tanks and the Canadians lost heavily.[30]

In VIII Corps the only major tasks for 20 July were the capture of Frenouville and Bourguebus. Frenouville, after a dawn attack by the RAF, was easily captured by the Guards Armoured Division, and the 7th took Bourguebus with little more trouble. Several counterattacks were launched but the Germans were beaten off and numerous prisoners taken. Then, at 1600, a torrential rain began to fall and all operations ground to a halt. The Battle for Bourguebus Ridge was over.

At 1000 the next morning, VIII Corps with its three armoured divisions relinquished responsibility

---

30. Stacey, *Victory Campaign*, pp. 175-76.

for any part of the front line, which now belonged to II Canadian Corps. The 11th Armoured Division was completely withdrawn to refit, while the other divisions were to be a reserve for the Canadians. By this time the Germans were as unable and unwilling to launch a major offensive as were the British. In six hours the three armoured divisions had driven on to Bourguebus Ridge, and after two more days of fighting the position was consolidated. This forced the Germans to move in massive reinforcements to ensure that the attack would not gain any more ground.

CHAPTER VII

The Threat is Mounted

OPERATION GOODWOOD was over. Now came the critiques, the evaluations, and the bitter feuds over the results, along with further fighting around the Goodwood salient. There were two basic controversies about the operation, both of which have survived to the present. The first is over the real result of the battle: Was it a success or a failure—did the British inflict a defeat on the Germans or did the British in fact suffer a defeat? Coupled with these thoughts, are questions involving the intentions of Montgomery and the British in regard to this operation: Was it the big breakout or just an attack with local objectives and a strategic purpose? Directly affected by these answers but continuing regardless of the correct answers, was the dispute at the highest levels over whether Montgomery had failed to

Mounting the Threat

accomplish what he had promised to do or if he had deliberately lied to the Americans and the Royal Air Force to get what he wanted for Operation Goodwood.

The answers are difficult to discover at this late date. More materials are becoming available, but fewer survivors are living to comment on them. In addition, with each succeeding year, the opinions expressed in print seem to take on more validity because of longevity and because of their repeated use by the hasty author anxious to support what more prominent authors have previously written.

The answers that can be discerned from the materials available are generally favorable to Montgomery and pro-British. Goodwood was a success. With the 11th Armoured Division charge on 18 July, the British made the biggest single gain since the Invasion. By the use of air power and armoured vehicles, they had accomplished this with a minimal loss of life and at the same time inflicted heavy damage on the Germans who were suffering from earlier heavy losses.

It is also clear that from inception to conclusion, Goodwood was an attack with limited objectives. At no level, from 21st Army Group to 11th Armoured Division, was the planning concerned with a major breakthrough as an integral part of the operation. Obviously, the planners had to take into account the possibility of finding themselves suddenly confronted with a breakthrough that would have to be exploited, but they did not plan that it would happen. This brings us to the question of General Montgomery and what he said. Montgomery undoubtedly emphasized this operation as being of great importance. Indeed, within his concept of the Normandy campaign, it was significant, for it set up the great breakthrough that was to come later in the month of July and lead to the great victory at Falaise in August.

I do think, however, that Montgomery may well have overemphasized the operation to the Royal Air Force in order to get the air support that he needed. The RAF was definitely reluctant to support the army and, without the authority to order the tasks done, Montgomery did have to "sell" Goodwood. But I do not think that Montgomery really oversold the operation to any degree. Much of the antagonism appears to come from personal dislikes within the higher echelons and from an inability or unwillingness to understand the intentions and results of Goodwood.

Before continuing the discussion of the controversy surrounding Goodwood, the final battles on Bourguebus Ridge must be described. After the rainstorm and the relief of VIII Corps, the Bourguebus Ridge front remained relatively quiet until 25 July. On that morning the Canadians, who were now responsible for the area, launched Operation Spring.[1] This was a two-division attack directly down the Falaise road in an attempt to take the area up to Rocquancourt, including la Hogue, Verrieres, Tilly-la-Campagne, and Garcelles-Secqueville, and to maintain the threat of a major breakthrough on this flank. In fact Montgomery seemed to have contem-

---

1. C. P. Stacey, *The Victory Campaign*, pp. 186-96.

plated another Goodwood-type operation.[2] However, because of the success of Goodwood, the great bulk of the German armour was on the Canadian front and so Spring was a failure. It did serve a useful purpose in confusing the Germans as to whether or not Operation Cobra, the major attack launched on the American front at the same time, was really the main thrust.

This American attack was, indeed, the right-hand swing that Montgomery and Bradley had spoken of, and it was to be a very successful breakout from the American front. This was the payoff of Montgomery's strategy: he had drawn the Germans to his flank and battered them in battle, now the Americans could mount a massive attack against minimal armoured opposition in the St. Lo-Avranches area. Once this offensive began to show major success, the German armoured division began to leave the British/Canadian front and move to the threatened American front.

Now the Canadians could attack once again along the ridge. The next operation, called Totalize, on 7–11 August, finally took the remainder of the Goodwood villages and moved the front line down the ridge almost to Potigny, nearly eleven miles further.[3] This was quickly followed by Operation Tractable which brought the Canadians to the outskirts of Falaise and then to the destruction of the surrounded Germans at the battle of the Falaise Gap.[4]

When the American attack began on 25 July,

---

2. *Ibid.*, p. 183.
3. *Ibid.*, pp. 216-31.
4. *Ibid.*, pp. 236-66.

Hitler had ordered a massive counterattack in a vain attempt to hold the onslaught. This left the remnants of two German armies to be trapped and crushed between the encircling Allied forces. Montgomery's strategy was wildly successful. As a result of his plan of blows from each flank alternately hitting the Germans, and his drawing of the German armour to the British flank as a result of Goodwood, Montgomery was able to set up the Germans for this defeat—with a little help from Hitler.

But immediate results are the basis upon which people generally rate success or failure. The immediate results of Operation Goodwood were the establishment of three British armoured divisions on Bourguebus Ridge, the capture of the suburbs of Caen, the great expansion of the salient across the Orne, and the capture or destruction of large numbers of German tanks, guns and personnel. These events in turn caused the Germans to make major readjustments in the location of their armoured forces.

Losses of weapons and personnel are a major criterion used to assess the results of a battle. The figures most generally quoted as a measure of success or failure are tank losses. The figures for Goodwood range from the 500 of an official and rather biased American historian[5] to the technically correct but misleading 139 of this author. To some extent the figure one uses depends on what one is trying to prove: the higher losses an author lists, the better chance he has

---

5. Martin Blumenson, *Breakout and Pursuit*, p. 193.

of proving the British were defeated. To understand the situation, let us start with the total strength involved. The British armoured division had a basic tank strength of roughly 343 at full war establishment.[6] This was predicated on 61 cruiser tanks per regiment, but records show that 53 or 54 would be more accurate for the regiments participating in Goodwood.[7] The total figure also includes 8 observation-post tanks with no guns, 25 anti-aircraft tanks with light anti-aircraft guns, 18 tanks in brigade or division headquarters, and 63 light tanks of questionable value.[8] Therefore, two different figures can be calculated. With the total strength of the three armoured divisions, there might have been 1,029 tanks (343 times 3) on the plains below Bourguebus Ridge. On the other hand, there were not more than 738 cruiser tanks and, assuming 50 cruiser tanks to a regiment (with four regiments in the division, and three divisions in the corps), probably not more than 600.

Determining when a tank is really destroyed is also a vexing problem. Tanks can stop on the battlefield for any of a great number of reasons. They can stall, throw a piston, drop a track, stick in the mud, take a direct hit from an 88, or hit a mine; and tanks did all of these things in Goodwood. Even when a tank had been hit by an 88 it was not necessarily destroyed. The shell could break a track, knock off a road wheel or

---

6. H. F. Joslen, *Orders of Battle, Second World War, Volume 1*, p. 9.
7. R. J. B. Sellar, *The Fife and Forfar Yeomanry 1919–1956*, p. 170.
8. Joslen, p. 9.

drive sprocket, penetrate and destroy the engine, or penetrate the turret and set off the ammunition totally destroying the tank. Thus, the casualty figures for Goodwood must be carefully examined. Most authors who treat the subject suggest that roughly two-thirds of the tanks that stopped on any one day were battle casualties and one-third were driving casualties. Of the battle casualties, roughly one-half would be recoverable, i.e., not burned or blown up.[9] About one-half of the losses could be repaired, whether battle casualties or driving casualties.[10] Therefore, many of the tanks lost on the first day were back in action on the second day. As an example, in the Fife and Forfar, fifty-three tanks were operational at the beginning of Goodwood and forty-three were "knocked out" on the first day, but on the morning of the nineteenth, there were twenty-five tanks available.[11] There would have been more if some had not been destroyed in the bombing of the rear echelons as they were being repaired.

In dealing with the figures, the author assumes that they only apply to cruiser tanks and that they are raw, i.e., representing all tanks out of action, because in the few cases where information is available that is the situation.[12] In the 11th Armoured Division, 126 tanks were out of action: 26 in the 23rd Hussars, 41 in the 3rd Royal Tanks, 43 in the Fife and Forfar, and

---

9. Chester Wilmot, *The Struggle for Europe*, p. 360.
10. General Adair, June 1971: talk at the battlefield tour; Sellar, p. 171; G. S. Jackson, *Operations Eighth Corps*, p. 102.
11. Sellar, p. 171.
12. Jackson, p. 102.

16 in the Northamptonshire Yeomanry.[13] In the Guards Armoured Division 60 were stopped,[14] and an unknown but small number in the 7th. On the second day, the 11th lost another 65 and the losses in the other divisions are unknown.[15] Thus, on the first day about 200 tank casualties occurred of which perhaps 100 could be repaired, and on the second day probably 70 to 80 of which about 40 could be repaired. Of those that could be repaired, not all were in action the next day but were within a short time. On the third day, no tanks were destroyed in the armoured divisions, for the 11th was in reserve and the others were singularly lucky. Thus, by common sense, we arrive at a figure of 140 tanks destroyed (the actual figure is 139): 100 in the 11th, 30 in the Guards and 9 in the 7th.[16] In addition, 18 were stopped in the 3rd Division attacks near Troarn, where the 27th Armoured Brigade was in action.[17] Therefore, the three-day total was probably about 300 tanks stopped for all causes and 140 to 150 tanks actually destroyed, not including light tanks etc. Out of a total of 650 tanks, this is a staggering loss.

---

13. *Ibid*. However, these figures do not satisfactorily explain the possibility of other losses. Surely some light tanks and others were casualties. For example, in W. Brownlie Steele, *Proud Trooper*, p. 377, the 151st Field Regiment, Royal Artillery had two tank casualties among its O.P. tanks. One was destroyed and the other damaged but recoverable.
14. General Adair.
15. Stacey, *Victory Campaign*, p. 170; B. H. Liddell Hart, *The Tanks. Volume II*, p. 368.
16. Liddell Hart, p. 369.
17. L. F. Ellis, *Victory in the West: Vol. I. The Battle of Normandy*, p. 343.

It should be remembered, however, that few actual crew casualties occurred in Goodwood. In the Fife and Forfars, which lost 43 tanks from all causes, there were 66 personnel casualties, of whom 35 were killed or missing.[18] In the 4th King's Shropshire Light Infantry, one of the infantry battalions that saw far less combat, 100 were killed, wounded and missing.[19] In the three armoured divisions on 18 July, there were 521 casualties; while in the total operation for that day there were 1,500,[20] equalling roughly 1,000 to be shared by the four brigades on the left flank—three from the 3rd division and one from the 51st Highland—and the six brigades of the 2nd and 3rd Canadian Divisions. While many authors claim that the use of tanks and bombing cut down enormously on casualties,[21] in absolute terms, each brigade committed suffered about the same number per unit. However, the armoured units did capture a great deal more territory for the same expenditure in lives. It also must be remembered that at this time the British were extremely short of infantry replacements, so that even from the melancholy aspects of casualties, the operation was a success.

The Germans had also suffered: 21st and 1st SS Panzer Divisions lost 109 tanks on the eighteenth.[22] German tank losses unlike British were generally physically lost, falling into the hands of the enemy,

---

18. Sellar, p. 170.
19. P. K. Kemp, *The History of the 4th Battalion, The King's Own Shropshire Light Infantry (T.A.) 1745–1945*, p. 93.
20. Ellis, *Victory in the West*, p. 345.
21. For example, Liddell Hart, p. 369.
22. G. L. Verney, *The Guards Armoured Division*, p. 45.

with the exception of those put out of action by the RAF in rear areas. The Germans also lost 2,500 prisoners to the British and, if that figure is any indication, at least that many must have been killed and wounded, for a total, in all three corps, of at least 5,000 casualties. Third British Infantry Division felt that there were at least 2,000 German casualties on its front alone.[23]

The most adverse effect on the Germans was that by the afternoon of the eighteenth massive German reinforcements were diverted from important tasks. The 21st Panzer Division and 1st SS Panzer Division were in the immediate area and so were involved, but the Germans also hurriedly sent the 116th and 12th SS Panzer Divisions to support the defenders of the ridge along with elements of the 2nd Panzer Division and eventually of the 9th SS Panzer Division. By 24 July, seven Panzer divisions and four heavy-tank battalions faced the British, while only two Panzer divisions and a Panzer grenadier division faced the Americans. While the Canadians suffered in Operation Spring from this imbalance of enemy troops, the Germans suffered more as a result in Cobra. In my opinion, this is what really made Goodwood a success. The sacrifices of the three armoured divisions had drawn the enemy from the real danger point, St. Lo, to the British flank.

Having evaluated the gains and losses of the operation, we return to the criticism of Montgomery. There are three bodies of criticism against Montgomery over Operation Goodwood. The first is that of his

---

23. Norman Scarfe, *Assault Division*, p. 123.

professional contemporaries, primarily General Bradley and Air Marshal Tedder; the second is that of writers of the time, most notably Ralph Ingersoll and Harry Butcher; and finally that of the modern historians who follow the paths laid out by their predecessors.

Air Marshal Sir Arthur Tedder may be considered the great starting point of the Goodwood controversy. On 20 July he telephoned Eisenhower and expressed his disappointment over the slowness of the battle. His conversation and actions at the time were recorded by Captain Harry Butcher, the naval aide to Eisenhower and not one of Montgomery's great admirers.[24] In Butcher's version, Tedder states that "the British Chiefs of Staff would support any recommendation that Ike might care to make with respect to Monty for not succeeding in going places with his big three-armoured-division push. . . . The air people are completely disgusted with the lack of progress."[25] Butcher then goes on to make a very perceptive comment:

> It is really one of those symptoms of the chronic rivalry between the air and ground, fanned by the resentment of many British Army and Air officers, particularly those who served in the desert, because Monty has not learned the art of giving credit to all services and commanders for his past victories.[26]

---

24. Captain Harry C. Butcher, *My Three Years with Eisenhower*.
25. *Ibid.*, p. 617.
26. *Ibid.*, p. 618.

He then implies that the British want to, and should, "kick 'Monty' upstairs," and also that Eisenhower was thinking of doing something. "Ike is like a blind dog in a meat house—he can smell it, but he can't find it."[27] Butcher does not help the validity of his reporting by incorrectly describing Goodwood and one of the units involved.[28] Tedder himself, in his autobiography, *With Prejudice*, denies the statements Butcher makes, but says, "On 20 July, I spoke to Portal (Air Chief Marshal Sir Charles Portal) about the Army's failure. We were agreed in regarding Montgomery as the cause."[29] Tedder also implies that the idea of a breakout on the American front was then formulated by Bradley behind Montgomery's back, because Montgomery would not do it on the British front.

Much of this controversy was in existence before Goodwood as a result of Montgomery's failure to secure the airfield sites that the air forces thought so important. Hence much of this high-level hostility had been revealed before, for example, after Operation Windsor.

Bradley is in an ambiguous position. He says in one place, "Montgomery was spending his reputation in a bitter seige against the old university city of Caen"; many writers have seized on this statement as a further condemnation of Montgomery. But in the next few lines, he shows the true situation. "In this

---

27. *Ibid.*, p. 619.
28. *Ibid.*, p. 617. Butcher mentions the "Scots' 5th Brigade" possibly meaning the 51st (Highland) Division which took over part of the front.
29. Marshal of the Royal Air Force Lord Tedder, *With Prejudice*, p. 562.

diversionary mission Monty was more than successful, for the harder he hammered towards Caen the more German troops he drew into that sector." Bradley further says, "Had we attempted to exonerate Montgomery by explaining how successfully he had hoodwinked the Germans we would have also given our strategy away."[30] This adds a new dimension to the situation: perhaps the whole thing was a successful plot to fool the Germans, that also fooled some people on the British side.

It is particularly ironic for Bradley to be used as evidence against Montgomery, since it was Bradley's inability to breakout that led the British commander to undertake Goodwood in order to divert the Germans until the Americans were ready. And it was the absence of German armour that allowed Bradley his success in Cobra.

The most virulent criticism came from those on the fringes of the official circle—correspondents and ex-correspondents connected with the Allied headquarters. The most outstanding example of this is Ralph Ingersoll in *Top Secret*. "He [Montgomery] was stopped just beyond Caen after practically destroying the British Armoured Corps by running his tanks in successive head-on charges into German 88 fire. He failed to destroy, or even to defeat, the German army opposite him."[31] Ingersoll then warms to his task:

> Most of all, however, it was the hedgerow country that lost Montgomery the battle of

---
30. Omar N. Bradley, *A Soldier's Story*, p. 325.
31. Ralph Ingersoll, *Top Secret*, p. 162.

Caen—the hedgerow country that beat the men who had learned their trade on the flat desert. The hedgerows won over the individual courage and brilliance of soldiers who had survived Africa because they were both brave and brilliant but who did not understand the terrain in which they now fought.

This I know from personal observation because at the conferences that planned the battle of Caen the minority opinion (led by a young American colonel named Bonesteel) predicted what would happen to armour in hedgerow country but was overruled.[32]

Ingersoll uses this argument to show that the Americans are obviously cleverer than the out-of-date desert warriors and to show clearly why the British tanks were defeated outside of Caen; however, he overlooks one minor detail. The hedgerows, the bocage of Normandy, are a considerable distance from Bourguebus Ridge, and although 7th Armoured Division had received a setback in the bocage in early June, this was not the battle that Ingersoll is discussing when he talks of "the back of British armor . . . being broken at Caen."[33]

Newspaper correspondents were also in the forefront of criticism against Montgomery. Many headlines indicated that the Normandy front was bogged

---

32. *Ibid.*, p. 163. The context makes clear that these remarks apply to Goodwood.
33. *Ibid.*

down and that claims by the higher commanders were exaggerated. This obviously had a great effect on public opinion and influenced writers, especially the later writers who had to rely on published sources. Martin Blumenson in his official history on this period uses exaggerated loss figures to imply failure, describes those who take Montgomery's side as apologists, and lists the complaints against Montgomery without listing the defenses offered.[34] Alexander McKee in his book *Last Round Against Rommel* also takes an anti-Montgomery slant by claiming that Dempsey had a much broader plan in mind, including Falaise, but that Montgomery had stopped him.[35] In view of the supply, and especially the manpower, situations of the British, if Montgomery did indeed (and there is no evidence that he did) prevent Dempsey from trying a larger plan, it was because Montgomery had a clearer picture of the realities of the British situation.

These works seem to cover the complete spectrum of complaints about Montgomery. First, that he promised more than he could deliver from the operation, and, secondly, that he was too cautious in his execution of the plan, to the point of stopping the armour unnecessarily as McKee and Ingersoll imply. In answer to the first, I think the planning information presented in Chapters I through III makes it clear that this was only to be a limited attack, with, of course, the possibility of a breakthrough. It is my

---

34. Blumenson, p. 195.
35. Alexander McKee, *Last Round Against Rommel: Battle of the Normandy Beachhead* (New York: Signet Books, 1966) p. 258.

opinion that Montgomery overemphasized the importance of Goodwood to insure adequate air support. As to the second complaint, I think it is obvious from the battle itself and the histories of the units that Montgomery did not halt British armour prematurely on Bourguebus Ridge. They may have been stopped prematurely, but it was because of German resistance and British slowness, and not because of Montgomery.

I would suggest that most critics of Goodwood are unable or unwilling to view the battle within the context of the strategic situation. There seems to be a belief that every individual battle is either a tremendous success or a total failure. Operation Goodwood achieved a great deal, and if it did not achieve its exact territorial objectives or defeat the entire German army, it was still as effective as many battles of the Second World War that are acclaimed as successes.

Operation Goodwood achieved its strategic goals by its effect on the dispositions of German armour, and it did move British forces onto Bourguebus Ridge, although not in the exact positions desired. It also caused enormous destruction of the German troops in that area. The operation must be counted a success. It was a prelude to victory in that it enabled the Allies to set up the victory at Falaise, and thus begin the dash across France and Belgium which so quickly liberated those countries.

APPENDIX A

Allied Chain of Command

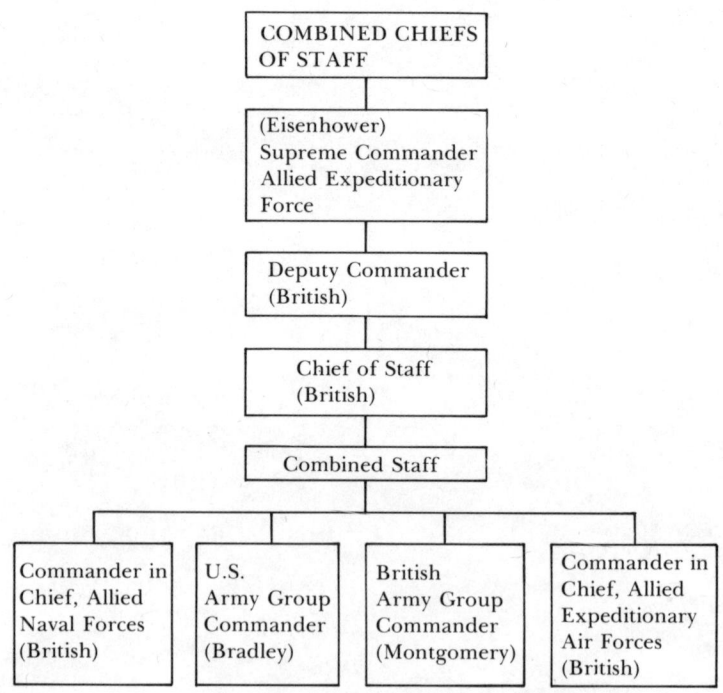

APPENDIX B

Allied Formations

Supreme Headquarters, Allied Expeditionary Force
  General Dwight D. Eisenhower
Army Group or Air Force
Army-with Army Troops and Army Group Royal Artillery
  (AGRA)
Corps
├─────────────────┬─────────────────┤
Division   Separate Brigades   Separate Regiments

Forces of Great Britain and the Commonwealth:

ARMY GROUP LEVEL

   21st Army Group—General Sir Bernard Montgomery

ARMY LEVEL

Second British Army—Lt. General Sir Miles Dempsey
First Canadian Army still in Britain

CORPS LEVEL

First Corps—Lieutenant-General J. T. Crocker
Eighth Corps—Lieutenant-General Sir Richard O'Connor
Second Canadian Corps—Lieutenant-General G. G. Simonds

DIVISION LEVEL

I Corps:

6th Airborne Division—Major-General R. N. Gale
  3rd Parachute Brigade
    8th and 9th Parachute Battalions
    1st Canadian Parachute Battalion
  5th Parachute Brigade
    7th, 12th and 13th Battalions The Parachute Regiment
  6th Airlanding Brigade
    12th Bn. The Devonshire Regt.
    2nd Bn. The Oxfordshire and Buckinghamshire Light Infantry

3rd Division—Major-General L. G. Whistler
  8th Brigade
    1st Bn. the Suffolk Regt.
    2nd Bn. the East Yorkshire Regt.
    1st Bn. the South Lancashire Regt.
  9th Brigade
    2nd Bn. the Lincolnshire Regt.
    1st Bn. the King's Own Scottish Borderers
    2nd Bn. the Royal Ulster Rifles
  185th Brigade
    2nd Bn. the Royal Warwickshire Regt.

Allied Formations / 127

    1st Bn. the King's Shropshire Light Infantry
    1st Bn. the Royal Norfolk Regt.

  51st (Highland) Division — Major-General D. C. Bullen-Smith
    152nd Brigade
      2nd and 5th Bn. the Seaforth Highlanders
      5th Bn. the Queens Own Cameron Highlanders
    153rd Brigade
      5th Bn. the Black Watch
      1st and 5th/7th Bn. the Gordon Highlanders
    154th Brigade
      1st and 7th Bn. the Black Watch
      7th Bn. the Argyll and Sutherland Highlanders
    2nd Derbyshire Yeomanry

VIII Corps

  Guards Armoured Division — Major-General A.H.S. Adair
    5th Guards Armoured Brigade
      2nd Bn. the Grenadier Guards
      1st Bn. the Coldstream Guards
      2nd Bn. the Irish Guards
      1st (Motor) Bn. the Grenadier Guards
    32nd Guards Brigade
      5th Bn. the Coldstream Guards
      3rd Bn. the Irish Guards
      1st Bn. the Welsh Guards
    2nd Armoured Reconnaissance Bn. the Welsh Guards

  7th Armoured Division—Major-General G. W.E.J. Erskine
    22nd Armoured Brigade
      4th County of London Yeomanry
      1st and 5th Bn. the Royal Tank Regiment
    131st Infantry Brigade
      1/5th, 1/6th, and 1/7th Bn. The Queen's Royal Regt.

8th King's Royal Hussars

11th Armoured Division—Major-General G.P.B. Roberts
  29th Armoured Brigade
    23rd Hussars
    3rd Bn. the Royal Tank Regiment
    2nd Fife and Forfar Yeomanry
    8th Bn. the Rifle Brigade (Motor)
  159th Infantry Brigade
    3rd Bn. the Monmouthshire Regt.
    4th Bn. the King's Own Shropshire Light Infantry
    1st Bn. the Herefordshire Regt.
  2nd Northamptonshire Yeomanry

II Canadian Corps

2nd Canadian Division—Major-General C. Foulkes
  4th Brigade
    The Royal Regiment of Canada
    The Royal Hamilton Light Infantry
    The Essex Scottish Regiment
  5th Brigade
    The Black Watch of Canada
    Le Regiment de Maisonneuve
    The Calgary Highlanders
  6th Brigade
    Les Fusiliers Mont-Royal
    The Queen's Own Cameron Highlanders of Canada
    The South Saskatchewan Regiment

3rd Canadian Division—Major-General R.F.L. Keller
  7th Brigade
    The Royal Winnepeg Rifles
    The Regina Rifle Regiment
    1st Bn. the Canadian Scottish Regt.
  8th Brigade
    The Queen's Own Rifles of Canada

Le Regiment de la Chaudiere
The North Shore (New Brunswick) Regt.
9th Brigade
   The Highland Light Infantry of Canada
   The Stormont, Dundas and Glengarry Highlanders
   The North Nova Scotia Highlanders

WAR ESTABLISHMENT OF BRITISH DIVISIONS

Armoured Division   343 tanks
   Armoured Reconnaissance Regiment 76 tanks
   HQ Armoured Brigade   10 tanks
      3 Armoured Regiments   72 tanks each
      Motor Bn.
   HQ Infantry Brigade
      3 Infantry Bn.
   HQ Division Royal Artillery
      2 Field Regt.   48 guns total
      1 Anti-Tank Regt.   48 guns

Infantry Division
   Reconnaissance Regt.
   3 HQ Brigades
      3 Infantry Bn. each
   HQ Division Royal Artillery
      2 field regts.
      1 anti-tank regt.

Armoured Division-14,964 personnel

Infantry Division-18,347 personnel

APPENDIX C

German Order of Battle

5th Panzer Armee (Panzergruppe West)
    General der Panzertruppe Heinrich Eberbach
1st SS Panzer Corps
    General der Panzertruppe Josef Dietrich
LXXXVI Corps
    General Erich Straube
1st SS Panzer Division
    Brigadefuhrer Theodor Wisch
12th SS Panzer Division
    Generalmajor der Waffen SS Kurt Meyer
21st Panzer Division
    Generalmajor Edgar Feuchtinger
272nd Infantry Division
    Generalleutnant Schack
346th Infantry Division
    Generaleutnant Erich Diestel
16th Luftwaffe Field Division
    Generalleutnant Karl Sievers

APPENDIX D

Weapon Comparison

Weapons	Muzzle Velocity	Armour Penetration
Tank guns:		
75 mm. (British)	2,050 fps	60mm at 1,000 yds.
75 mm. (German)	2,460 fps	84mm at 1,000 yds.
17 pounder (British)	N/A	130mm at 1,000 yds.
88 mm. Tank (German)	N/A	102mm at 1,000 yds.
88mm. AA (German)	3,280 fps	168mm at 1,000 yds. (also in latest Tigers)

Tanks	Gun	Speed	Armour (Frontal)
Honey	37mm	40 mph	44mm
Sherman	75mm	24 mph	76mm
Cromwell	75mm	40 mph	75mm
Mark IV (21st Pz Div)	75mm	25 mph	80mm
Panther (1st SS Pz Div)	75mm	34 mph	100mm
Tiger I (503rd SS Heavy Tank Bn.)	88mm Tank	23 mph	100mm
Tiger II (503rd SS Heavy Tank Bn.)	88mm AA	25 mph	180mm

Bibliography

SOURCES CITED IN TEXT

The Administrative History of the Operations of 21 Army Group on the Continent of Europe, 6 June 1944–8 May 1945. Germany: British Army of the Rhine, 1945.
Battlefield Tour: Operation Goodwood. Pamphlet prepared by the Staff College, Camberley.
Belfield, Eversley, and H. Essame. *The Battle for Normandy.* London: B. T. Batsford, Ltd., 1965.
Bell, Capt. T. J. *Into Action with the 12th Field.* N.P. N.D.
Blumenson, Martin. *Breakout and Pursuit.* Washington: Office of the Chief of Military History, 1961.
Bradley, Omar N. *A Soldier's Story.* New York: Henry Holt and Co., 1951.
Bridging: Normandy to Berlin. British Army of the Rhine, 1945.
British Army of the Rhine-Battlefield Tour. First Day. 8 Corps Operations East of the Orne, 18–21 July 1944. (Operation Goodwood). Prepared under the direction of G (Trg), HQ British Army of the Rhine, June 1947.

Butcher, Captain Harry C. *My Three Years with Eisenhower*. New York: Simon & Schuster, 1946.
Churchill, Winston S. *The Second World War: Closing the Ring*. Boston: Houghton Mifflin, 1951.
De Guingand, Major General Sir Francis. *Operation Victory*. New York: Charles Scribner's Sons, 1947.
Eisenhower, Dwight D. *Crusade in Europe*. Garden City: Doubleday & Co., 1948.
Ellis, L. F. *Victory in the West: Volume I. The Battle of Normandy*. London: Her Majesty's Stationery Office, 1962.
Ellis, L. F. *Welsh Guards at War*. Aldershot: Gale and Polden, 1946.
Erskine, D. H. *The Scots Guards*. London: Clowes, 1956.
FitzGerald, Major D.J.L. *History of the Irish Guards in the Second World War*. Aldershot: Gale & Polden, 1949.
Foreign Military Studies. Mss. B-284, p. 1328-36. "Die Zerschlagung der 16. Lw. Feld Div. am 18. 7. 44. Sudostw. Caen." by Generalleutnant Karl Sievers.
History of 7th Armoured Division June 1943–July 1945. British Army of the Rhine. N.D.
Howard, Michael and John Sparrow. *The Coldstream Guards 1920–1946*. London: Oxford University Press, 1951.
Ingersoll, Ralph. *Top Secret*. New York: Harcourt Brace, 1946.
Jackson, G. S. *Operations Eighth Corps*. London: St. Clements. N.D.
Jenner, Martin. *Die 216/272 niedersachsische Infanterie-Division 1939–1945*. Bad Neuheim: Podzun Verlag, 1964.
Joslen, H. F. *Orders of Battle, Second World War. Volume I*. London: Her Majesty's Stationery Office, 1960.
Kemp, Lieut.-Comdr. P. K. *The History of the 4th Battalion, The King's Own Shropshire Light Infantry (T.A.) 1745-1945*. Shrewsbury: Wilding and Sons, 1955.
Liddell Hart, B. H. *The Tanks. Volume II*. London: Cassell, 1959.
McKee, Alexander, *Caen, the Anvil of Victory*. London: Souvenir Press, 1964.
McKee, Alexander, *Last Round Against Rommel: Battle of the Normandy Beachhead*. New York: Signet Books, 1966.
MacMillan, Captain Norman. *The Royal Air Force in the World War. Volume IV*. London: George G. Harrap, 1950.
Meyer, Kurt. *Grenadiere*. Munchen-Lochausen: Schild-Verlag, 1957.
Montgomery of Alamein, Field Marshal the Viscount. *The Memoirs of Field Marshal Montgomery*. New York: Signet Books, 1959.

Montgomery of Alamein, Field Marshal the Viscount. *Normandy to the Baltic.* Boston: Houghton Miflin Co., 1948.
Morgan, Lieutenant General Sir Fredrick. *Overture to Overlord.* London: Hodder and Stoughton, Ltd., 1947.
Munro, Ross. *Gauntlet to Overlord.* Toronto: The MacMillan Company of Canada, 1946.
Nicholson, Nigel and Patrick Forbes. *The Grenadier Guards in the War of 1939–1945. Volume I.* Aldershot: Gale and Polden, 1949.
Rosse, Captain the Earl and Colonel E. R. Hill. *The Story of the Guards Armoured Division.* London: Geoffrey Bles, 1956.
Salmond, J. B. *The History of the 51st Highland Division 1939–1945.* Edinburgh: William Blackwood, 1953.
Saunders, Hilary St. G. *Royal Air Force 1939–1945. Volume III. The Fight is Won.* London: Her Majesty's Stationery Office, 1954.
Scarfe, Norman. *Assault Division.* London: Collins, 1947.
Sellar, R.J.B. *The Fife and Forfar Yeomanry 1919–1956.* Edinburgh: William Blackwood and Sons, 1960.
Stacey, Colonel C. P. *Canada's Battle in Normandy.* Ottawa: King's Printer, 1946.
Stacey, Colonel C. P. *The Victory Campaign.* Ottawa: Queen's Printer, 1966.
Steele, W. Brownlie. *The Proud Trooper.* London: Collins, 1964.
The Story of the Twenty-Third Hussars 1940–1946. The Regiment, 1946.
Taurus Pursuant, A History of 11th Armoured Division. N.P. N.D.
Tedder, Marshal of the Royal Air Force, Lord. *With Prejudice.* Boston: Little, Brown and Co., 1966.
Thompson, R. W. *Montgomery. The Field Marshal.* New York: Charles Scribner's Sons, 1969.
Twenty-fifth Field Regiment, Royal Artillery, Northwest Europe 1944–1945. Aldershot: Gale and Polden, 1948.
Verney, Major General G. L. *The Desert Rats.* London: Hutchinson, 1954.
Verney, Major General G. L. *The Guards Armoured Division.* London: Hutchinson, 1955.
Wilmot, Chester. *The Struggle for Europe.* New York: Harper and Row, 1952.

OTHER SOURCES

Ambrose, Stephen E. *The Supreme Commander: The War Years of General Dwight D. Eisenhower*. Garden City: Doubleday and Co., 1970.

Blumenson, Martin. *The Duel for France*. Boston: Houghton Mifflin, 1963.

Blumentritt, Guenther. *Von Rundstedt*. London: Odhams, 1952.

Bryant, Arthur. *Triumph in the West*. Garden City: Doubleday and Co., 1959.

Carrel, Paul. *Invasion-They're Coming*. New York: Dutton, 1963.

Churchill, Winston S. *The Second World War: Triumph and Tragedy*. Cambridge: Houghton Mifflin, 1953.

De Guingand, Major General Sir Francis. *Generals at War*. London: Hodder and Stoughton, 1964.

Ehrman, John. *Grand Strategy: Volume V. August 1943–September 1944*. London: Her Majesty's Stationery Office, 1956.

Eisenhower, Dwight D. *Eisenhower's Own Story of the War*. New York: Arco Publishing Co., 1946.

Farran, Major Roy. *The History of the Calgary Highlanders 1921–1954*. Calgary: Bryant Press, 1954.

Fergusson, Bernard. *The Black Watch and the King's Enemies*. New York: Crowell, 1950.

Fernyhough, Brigadier A. H. *History of the Royal Army Ordnance Corps 1920–1945*. London: Royal Army Ordnance Corps. N.D.

Florentin, Eddy. *Battle of the Falaise Gap*. London: Elek Books, 1965.

Graham, Andrew. *Sharpshooters at War*. London: Sharpshooters Regimental Association, 1964.

Harrison, G. A. *Cross Channel Attack*. Washington: Office of the Chief of Military History, 1951.

Historical Records of the Queen's Own Cameron Highlanders. Volume IV. 1932–1948. Edinburgh: William Blackwood and Sons, 1952.

Jones, A. J. *The Second Derbyshire Yeomanry*. Bristol: White Swan Press, 1949.

Martin, Lieutenant General H. G. *The History of the Fifteenth Scottish Division 1939–1945*. Edinburgh: William Blackwood and Sons, 1948.

Miles, Wilfred. *The Life of a Regiment: Volume V. The Gordon Highlanders 1919–1945*. Aberdeen: The University Press, 1961.

North, John. *North-west Europe 1944–45*. London: Her Majesty's Stationery Office, 1953.

Oates, Lieutenant Colonel L. B. *Proud Heritage, The Story of the Highland Light Infantry. Volume IV. 1919–1959.* Glasgow: The House of Grant, 1963.

Orde, Roden. *The Household Cavalry at War: Second Household Cavalry Regiment.* Aldershot: Gale and Polden, 1953.

Pereira, Captain J. *A Distant Drum.* Aldershot: Gale and Polden, 1948.

Saunders, Hilary St. G. *The Red Beret.* London: Michael Joseph, 1950.

Schulman, Milton. *Defeat in the West.* New York: Dutton, 1948.

Sixsmith, Major General E.K.G. *British Generalship in the Twentieth Century.* London: Arms and Armour Press, 1970.

Smyth, Sir John. *Bolo Whistler.* London: Fredrick Muller, 1967.

Speidel, Hans. *We Defended Normandy.* London: Herbert Jenkins, 1951.

Index

Adair, Major General A.H.S., 59, 67
Amfreville, 68, 78
Armoured Vehicles, Royal Engineers (AVREs), 79
Atlantic, Operation, 98

Banneville la Campagne, 44, 69, 97
Bayeux, 76
Benouville, 12
Blumenson, Martin, 121
Bois de Bavent, 21
Bourguebus Ridge, 1, 6, 14, 35-40, 43, 47, 51, 62, 68, 72-73, 75-76, 79, 99, 105-6, 109, 111-12, 120, 122
Bourguebus village, 14, 24, 39-40, 70, 73, 84, 86, 90, 104-5
Bradley, General Omar N., 2, 10, 15, 36, 110, 117-19
Bras, 69, 73, 86, 91, 98, 102, 104
Bretteville-sur-Laize, 24, 39-40, 72
Butcher, Captain Harry C., 2, 117-118

Cabourg, 45

Caen, 4, 6, 8, 10, 12-14, 17-21, 23-25, 28, 30, 34-37, 39-40, 42, 62, 65, 69, 72, 73, 76, 98, 100, 120
Cagny, 44, 69, 71, 73-74, 82-84, 86, 93-95
Canal de Caen, 68, 77
Carpiquet, 13, 19, 25, 27, 30
Caumont, 21-22
Charnwood, Operation, 13, 19, 28, 30, 33, 35, 62
Cheux, 24
Chicheboville, 74
Churchill, Winston S., 7
Cobra, Operation, 110, 116
Colombelles, 14, 69-70, 99
Cormelles, 14, 40, 42, 105
COSSAC (Chief of Staff to the Supreme Allied Commander) 3-4, 8
Cotentin, 4
Cramesnil, 70, 73-75
Crocker, Lieutenant General J.T., 14, 28
Cromwell tanks, 23, 53-55, 59
Cuverville, 14, 44, 69, 71-72, 76, 81, 97

Demouville, 44, 69, 72, 76, 81, 97
Dempsey, Lieutenant General Sir
  Miles, 14, 36-38, 42-43, 46, 121

Eisenhower, General Dwight D., 2,
  10, 28, 44, 117
Emieville, 69, 74, 82
Epsom, Operation, 13, 18-19,
  24-26, 29-30, 35, 76
Erskine, Major General G.W.E.J.,
  57, 67, 95
Evrecy, 24

Falaise, 6, 14-15, 34, 43, 69, 109-10
Faubourg de Vaucelles, 99
Firefly tank, 55, 87
Fleury sur Orne, 40, 42, 105
Four, 70, 75, 84, 86, 104-5
Franceville, 45
Frenouville, 69, 94-95, 102, 104-5

Garcelles, 43, 70, 109
Giberville, 44, 69, 73, 98-99
Goodwood, Operation, 1-3, 13, 15,
  30, 34-38, 43-45, 53, 56, 59, 61,
  64-65, 67, 69, 75-77, 81, 86-87,
  96, 98, 101, 107-13, 116, 118-19,
  122
Grentheville, 69, 84, 86, 91, 96

Honey tank, 55
Hubert Folie, 43, 70, 73, 86-87, 91,
  102, 104

Ifs, 70, 99, 105
Ingersoll, Ralph, 2, 117, 119, 120,
  121

La Campagne, 75
La Hogue, 70, 75, 109
Le Mesnil Frementel, 69-71, 73,
  75, 79, 91
Le Quai, 97
Le Poirier, 69, 86, 94, 102, 104
Lisieux, 6, 20
Louvigny, 100
Luck, Colonel Hans von, 64, 93

Manneville, 97, 98
McKee, Alexander, 121

Meyer, Generalmajor der Waffen
  SS Kurt, 29
Military Formations:
  First Army, U.S., 41
  Second British Army, 12, 35-38,
    41-42
  Fifth Panzer Armee, 23
  Eighth British Army, 7
  9th Army Air Force, 44
  21st Army Group, 12, 18, 22, 36,
    49, 67, 108
  Armeegruppe West, 34
  Panzergruppe West, 35, 101
  RAF Bomber Command, 28
  Corps:
    I British, 12, 14, 25, 28, 37,
      42, 96, 105
    II Canadian, 14, 37, 42, 72,
      99, 106
    VIII British, 14, 24-25, 37,
      39-40, 42-43, 68, 70, 77,
      90, 97-98, 105, 109
    XII British, 27, 42
    XXX British, 42
    1st SS Panzer, 25
    II SS Panzer, 26
  Armoured Divisions:
    6th, 55
    7th, 20, 22-23, 36, 54, 56, 58,
      67, 73, 75-76, 78, 89, 91,
      95-96, 99, 102, 104-5, 114,
      120
    11th, 24, 36, 53, 57, 67,
      70-76, 78, 83-84, 86, 89,
      91, 94-96, 101-2, 104, 106,
      108, 113-14
    Guards, 36, 53, 58-59, 67,
      73-74, 76, 78, 89, 91,
      93-96, 99, 102, 104-5, 114
    1st SS Panzer, 62, 87, 101,
      104, 115-16
    12th SS Panzer, 27, 29-30,
      116
    2nd Panzer, 23, 116
    21st Panzer, 13, 20-21, 62, 64,
      82, 87, 101, 104, 115-16
    116th Panzer, 116
    Panzer Lehr, 35
  Infantry Divisions:
    3rd British, 12, 17-18, 20-22,
      25, 29-30, 42, 97-98, 105,
      114-16

Index / 141

15th Scottish, 24
43rd, 24
50th British, 20-23
51st Highland, 20, 22-26, 35, 98, 115
59th, 29
6th British Airborne, 12, 18-20
2nd Canadian, 100, 115
3rd Canadian, 18, 20, 22, 25, 99, 115
16th Luftwaffe Field, 29, 39, 62, 82, 98, 101
272nd, 62, 100
346th, 62, 98
Armoured Brigades:
5th Guards, 73, 74, 93
22nd, 75, 96
27th, 114
29th, 70-74, 78, 82-83, 91
Infantry Brigades:
8th, 97
9th, 97-98
32nd Guards, 74, 94-95
131st, 75
159th, 71, 73-74, 81, 91, 96
152nd, 98
185th, 13, 97
4th Canadian, 100
5th Canadian, 100
7th Canadian, 99
8th Canadian, 99
9th Canadian, 99
Regiments:
Black Watch of Canada, 100
Coldstream Guards, 94, 104
1st Battalion, 94
3rd County of London Yeomanry, 22
4th County of London Yeomanry, 96
22nd Dragoons, 79
2nd Fife and Forfar Yeomanry, 71, 82, 84, 86, 91, 102, 104, 113, 115
Grenadier Guards, 93-94
1st Battalion, 93
2nd Battalion, 93
23rd Hussars, 81, 86, 91, 102, 113
Inns of Court Regiment, 72
4th Battalion, King's

Shropshire Light Infantry, 81-82, 91, 115
2nd Northamptonshire Yeomanry, 72, 81, 104, 114
Queen's Own Rifles of Canada, 99
Regina Rifle Regiment, 100
Rifle Brigade
1st Battalion, 23
8th Battalion, 71, 91
Royal Tank Corps, 58
Royal Tank Regiment
1st, 96
3rd, 71, 79, 82, 84, 86, 102, 104, 113
5th, 96
Welsh Guards, 104
1st Battalion, 95
2nd Armoured Reconnaissance Battalion, 74, 95
125th Panzergrenadier, 64, 82, 100
503rd SS Heavy Tank Battalion, 83, 93
Kampfgruppe Luck, 64, 82
31st Luftwaffe Jaeger, 30
Mondeville, 40
Montgomery, General Sir Bernard, 1-3, 7-10, 12-13, 15, 17, 21-22, 28, 31, 33-34, 36-42, 44, 46, 57, 107-11, 116-22
Morgan, Lieutenant General Sir Fredrick, 3, 8

O'Connor, Lieutenant General Sir Richard N., 37-38, 67-69, 89, 93, 96, 102, 104
Odon River, 13, 30, 35
Orne River, 4, 6, 9, 13, 20, 24, 28, 35, 39-40, 42-43, 68, 72-73, 98-100

Perch, Operation, 13, 18-21, 24, 26
Portal, Air Chief Marshal Sir Charles, 118
Potigny, 110

Quebec Conference, 6

Ranville, 12

Roberts, Major General G.P.B., 57-58, 67-68, 76, 81, 96, 102
Rocquancourt 70, 73, 109
Roosevelt, President Franklin, 7

Saint Andre sur Orne, 72, 105
Saint Honorine la Chardonerette, 24, 26, 35, 98
St. Lo, 4, 6
St. Sylvain, 72
Sannerville, 42, 44, 69, 97, 101
Schweppenburg, General der Panzertruppen Freiherr Geyr von, 35
Secqueville, 43, 70, 75, 109
Sherman tank, 53-55, 61
Simonds, Lieutenant General G.G., 14, 99
Soliers, 69, 84, 86, 91, 104-5
Spring, Operation, 109-10, 116

Tedder, Marshal of the Air Force Lord, 2, 117-18
Tilly la Campagne, 14, 70, 109
Tilly sur Seulles, 23-24, 76
Totalize, Operation, 110
Touffreville, 69, 97, 101
Tractable, Operation, 110
Troarn, 20, 42, 97, 101, 105, 114

Vaucelles, 14, 40, 42, 99, 100
Verrieres, 43, 70, 73, 99, 104-5, 109
Villers Bocage 21-23
Vimont, 24, 39-40, 43, 69, 72, 74, 93, 102
Vire River, 4, 6

Windsor, Operation, 13, 18-19, 27-29, 118